Shipping Container Homes

How to build a sustainable, environmentally friendly home from scratch, stop paying rent and live comfortably.

SW Prem Jaganu

TABLE OF CONTENTS

Introduction

Embracing a Sustainable Lifestyle

In the crucible of modern living, the concept of home has transformed. It is no longer just a shelter or a mere accumulation of rooms but a statement of one's values, a testament to one's commitment to the environment, and an active player in the sustainability movement. As architects, designers, and citizens of a world teetering on the brink of ecological upheaval, we are summoned to pioneer lifestyles that honor and preserve the delicate balance of nature. The advent of shipping container homes is a beacon of this sustainable ethos, a clarion call to those poised to shape a future where green living is not a luxury but a necessity.

Embracing a sustainable lifestyle through the lens of container homes involves a confluence of ecological consciousness and cutting-edge design. It is a journey that begins with the understanding that the choices we make in constructing our living spaces ripple outwards, impacting the environment, economies, and communities. In the heart of an architect thrives the dual desire for innovation and stewardship. Container homes emerge as a nexus of these aspirations, serving as a tangible manifestation of minimalist living and sustainable choices.

This ethos of sustainability permeates every facet of life, transcending the mere act of recycling or choosing eco-friendly products. It is an immersive experience, a philosophy that informs the way we live, work, and interact with our surroundings. As architects, the choice to live in and promote container homes stands as a personal manifesto of sustainable intent. These steel structures, once retired from their voyages across the seas, now embark on a more stationary but equally poignant journey — as the building blocks of sustainable, affordable, and flexible homes.

The path to sustainability is not just paved with good intentions but with tangible, measurable actions. Incorporating a shipping container into one's practice and personal life requires a profound understanding of the lifecycle of materials, the energy costs of construction, and the social implications of building practices. In urban landscapes, where the ecological footprint is amplified, the transformation of shipping containers into chic, eco-friendly homes is a bold statement of urban rejuvenation and resourceful ingenuity.

A sustainable lifestyle advocates for more than energy efficiency or reduced carbon emissions; it beckons for a paradigm shift in how we conceive the concept of space. Shipping container homes epitomize the efficiency of space utilization — a minimalist approach that challenges the traditional sprawl with compact, thoughtfully designed habitats. This minimalist approach does not merely reduce clutter in our living spaces but also clarifies our priorities and values, focusing on what is essential for well-being and comfort.

Living sustainably means embracing a life where each element is carefully considered for its environmental impact, from the procurement of materials to the long-term energy consumption of the home. Shipping container homes, inherently modular and reusable, offer a sustainable blueprint that can be replicated, adapted, and evolved. They encourage a life where adaptability and simplicity are not just embraced but celebrated.

By choosing a shipping container as a dwelling, one opts for a life less ordinary — a life that respects the bounds of nature and seeks to reduce the strain on our planet's resources. This lifestyle is not just about personal gain; it's a communal statement, an inspiration to peers and future generations that responsible living can be achieved without compromising on aesthetics, comfort, or innovation.

An architect who embodies this sustainable lifestyle becomes a torchbearer for an eco-conscious future. Building one's own container home serves as a showcase project, an example to clients and the community of what is possible when creativity merges with ecological responsibility. It stands as a testament to the belief that good design and green living go hand in hand and that sustainability is not just a feature but the very foundation upon which the home is built.

In essence, the commitment to a sustainable lifestyle through the embrace of container homes is a multidimensional pursuit. It reaches beyond personal benefit, extending its impact on the community and the larger ecosystem. It redefines luxury as a well-lived life that honors the environment and champions innovative solutions. It is a lifestyle choice that demands mindfulness, responsibility, and a forward-thinking spirit — qualities that will define the contours of tomorrow's habitats and the legacy of today's architectural vanguards.

Why Choose a Shipping Container Home?

In the tapestry of modern architecture, shipping container homes stand out as a revolutionary thread, weaving together innovation, sustainability, and efficiency. The choice to adopt such a home is far from a mere trend-following gesture; it's a deliberate step toward reimagining the way we interact with our living spaces, a reflection of an architectural and personal philosophy that prioritizes ingenuity and conscious living.

Architects are by nature creators, visionaries who see beyond the concrete reality to what could be. In the case of container homes, what could be is a living, breathing expression of modernity. This three-dimensional canvas invites its inhabitants to paint with broad strokes of environmental stewardship and bold innovation. For the forward-thinking architect, a shipping container is not just a receptacle of goods but a vessel for dreams, a foundational block in what could become a bastion of modern, minimalist living.

The elegance of the container home lies in its simplicity and its potential for transformation. A single container is a building block, a starting point that asks, "What can I become?" And it is within this question that the heart of the movement pulses. These homes provide an opportunity for architects to practice what they preach, to demonstrate to a world often skeptical of change that sustainability and beauty are not only compatible—they're essential partners.

This commitment to minimalism and sustainability is not an abstract concept; it's a response to the authentic challenges of contemporary urban living. Cities across the globe are becoming densifying, becoming more expensive, and demanding innovative approaches to housing that are both space- and cost-efficient. Container homes answer this call with aplomb. They are the embodiment of urban ingenuity, turning the challenge of limited space into an opportunity for creative expression. The architect, in this scenario, becomes a magician of sorts, transforming the mundane into the extraordinary, the overlooked into the coveted.

For the architect, living in such a home is a declaration, a statement that their professional and personal values are in lockstep. It is a choice that proclaims a commitment to a lifestyle that values resourcefulness, customization, and adaptability. In a world where every square foot counts and every design decision can have profound implications for the environment, the container home stands as a testament to what is possible when creativity meets consciousness.

Financial pragmatism plays a role in this choice as well. Amid escalating costs in the urban housing market, the shipping container home is a financially accessible alternative. It allows the architect to invest in innovation rather than square footage, in quality rather than quantity. This financial aspect is not trivial—it's a crucial factor that enables more architects to become pioneers in their field, to test theories of sustainable living in real time, and to create spaces that are as much about function as they are about formed.

The container home is not just an architectural project; it's a personal journey toward a sustainable ethos. It's about living in a space that reflects the architect's values, about demonstrating the viability of an alternative way of life that champions reduced ecological impact. For the architect, building and living in a container home is akin to curating a personal exhibition, one that showcases a commitment to practices that are as innovative as they are necessary.

This choice is, in essence, a bold stride into a future where architecture acknowledges its profound impact on the environment and where architects take a leading role in advocating for change. It's about setting a precedent, about establishing a living, breathing example of what the future of urban housing can look like.

Choosing to live in a shipping container home, then, is more than a personal or professional statement—it's a mosaic of ideals, a confluence of economic savvy, and a deep-seated belief in the role of architecture as a catalyst for sustainable innovation. It is an emblem of the contemporary architect's spirit, an intersection of life and work. Each container represents a building block of a more mindful, aesthetically fulfilling, and environmentally responsible future.

Chapter 1

The History of Container Homes

Origins of the Shipping Container

In the bustling ports of the 1950s, amidst the clatter and chaos of cargo handling, a revolution was stirring. It wasn't heralded by blaring trumpets but by the humble steel box—the shipping container. To understand the container home, one must first journey back to this transformative era when the shipping container began reshaping global trade.

This innovation's genesis can be traced to the visionary Malcolm McLean, a trucking entrepreneur who saw inefficiency in the break-bulk cargo system. Laborers would spend exhaustive hours loading and unloading goods piece by piece from trucks to ships and back again. McLean's insight led to the containerization concept, ensuring cargo could move seamlessly between trucks, trains, and ships without the need for direct handling of the products inside.

This was more than mere convenience. It was an economic and social metamorphosis. Containerization slashed shipping costs, fueled global trade, and sparked an industrial ballet that connected distant corners of the world with a choreographed efficiency never seen before. The adoption of standardized sizes—

chiefly, the 20-foot and 40-foot containers—became the linchpin in this new world order of cargo transport, codifying a language of trade that every nation could speak.

Yet, what does this have to do with architecture and the ambition of a mid-career architect seeking sustainable innovation? Everything. The shipping container's journey from sea to shore to service as a structural element is a narrative of repurposing and resilience. Architects, more than any other professionals, appreciate the poetry of transforming the mundane into the magnificent, of seeing the latent potential in the most prosaic of structures.

As the trade lanes burgeoned with container traffic, something intriguing happened. The cost of returning empty containers to their origin proved prohibitive. Thus, ports became unintended graveyards for these retired steel boxes. Herein lay the seed for another revolution—repurposing these abandoned containers into habitable spaces.

Initially, it was their robust, weather-resistant nature that made them appealing as makeshift offices on construction sites. But soon, their true potential began to dawn on visionaries in architecture. These were modular, stackable, and sustainable elements that could be reimagined into living spaces. The humble container was to become a cornerstone of modern, minimalist, and eco-conscious design.

This notion coincided with a burgeoning awareness of sustainability and the necessity for innovative approaches to living spaces, particularly in urban areas where traditional construction could be cost-prohibitive. The concept of upcycling—not merely recycling—began to take hold. To upcycle a shipping container was to give it a new lease of life. This living space had previously crossed oceans and now would nestle in the heart of a modern metropolis, embodying both a home and a statement.

The architectural community started to take note. Here was a solution that addressed multiple concerns: the surplus of unused containers, the need for affordable housing, and the ever-growing environmental consciousness. The steel box that had revolutionized trade was now poised to revolutionize architecture. Architects and builders began experimenting, innovating, and refining the concept of the container home.

For an architect in his prime, whose very ethos is woven around sustainability and innovation, the shipping container represents a palette of possibilities. It isn't just about the transformation of steel into a structure but also about the message it sends—a testament to a more sustainable lifestyle, innovation in the face of constraints, and the elegance of minimalism.

The shipping container home is more than a dwelling; it is a narrative of progress. It speaks to the journey from industrial objects to personalized habitats. It is a story that resonates with architects who see beyond the steel walls and recognize the container's soul, a symbol of their commitment to shaping the future of living spaces.

Thus, the shipping container, once the workhorse of the maritime industry, has transcended its role, morphing into a cultural icon of sustainable living. It's a story of transformation that continues to inspire architects and dreamers alike, providing a canvas for ingenuity and a framework for homes that not only promise shelter but also echo a more resounding call to sustainability and minimalism. It's this story that lays the foundation for what container homes have become—a symbol of architectural innovation and a testament to the adaptability of human ingenuity.

Evolution into Homes

The metamorphosis of shipping containers into homes is a testament to human ingenuity and the adaptive reuse of materials. As we trace the evolution of container architecture, it becomes clear that this movement is not just a trend but a profound shift in the way we think about space, resources, and the very concept of home.

After the initial use of shipping containers for storage and makeshift shelters, the early 2000s marked a significant shift. Architects and designers began to explore the container's potential in earnest, recognizing its inherent strength, durability, and modular nature as a groundbreaking resource for constructing residential dwellings.

The first container homes were modest – often single units outfitted with the bare essentials. They served as an emblem of countercultural living, symbolizing a departure from traditionalism. However, as the movement gained traction, these steel boxes' capacity for customization and scalability became glaringly apparent. They were no longer mere containers but building blocks for innovative housing.

Architects started experimenting with multiple containers, stacking them in various configurations to create more extensive and more complex designs. Pioneers in the field of container architecture began to surface, each bringing their unique perspective to this emerging discipline. Notable among them was Adam Kalkin, who, in the early 2000s, introduced the concept of "container chic," showing the world that container homes could be both functional and aesthetically pleasing.

With this evolution came the realization that container homes could provide solutions to broader issues. The global housing crisis called for affordable, efficient housing, and containers answered this call. Disaster relief efforts found a resource in containers due to their transportability and quick setup, exemplified by their use in the aftermath of catastrophes like Hurricane Katrina.

Urban areas, where space is at a premium, saw an opportunity in container homes. Innovative projects demonstrated how these structures could fit into narrow lots or infill spaces that would not accommodate traditional buildings, providing living space in densely populated cities without the footprint of conventional construction.

Container homes also resonated with those seeking a minimalist lifestyle. They epitomized the concept of "less is more" – a small, intentionally designed space that contained everything one needed and nothing more. This minimalist trend, which swept through the lifestyle choices of many urban dwellers, was perfectly embodied by the container home movement.

Sustainability became a cornerstone of the container home evolution. Repurposing a single 40-foot container recycles about 3,500 kilograms of steel and saves about 8,000 kilowatt-hours that would otherwise be spent melting down a similar amount of raw steel. Container homes started to incorporate green technologies such as solar panels, rainwater harvesting systems, and green roofs, further cementing their status as icons of eco-friendly living.

Architects and designers began to refine the aesthetics and functionality of container homes, making them not just sustainable and affordable but also stylish and comfortable. Interiors of container homes transformed from industrial to contemporary chic, with sleek lines and bright, open spaces. The addition of large glass windows, thoughtful insulation, and creative use of non-toxic materials addressed both the natural light and the climate control aspects, making these homes as livable as they were innovative.

The journey of the shipping container from a stark symbol of global trade to a beloved icon of sustainable architecture demonstrates how creativity can redefine the purpose of an object. For the modern architect, especially one with an eye on sustainability and innovation, container homes are not just a niche market but a dynamic field ripe with opportunities for exploration and expression.

The evolution into homes is not the end but rather a chapter in the ongoing story of shipping containers. Each container home built is a personal and professional statement, a physical manifestation of the values of minimalism, sustainability, and ingenuity that are increasingly important in our fast-paced, resource-conscious world. This evolution is a narrative that continues to inspire, challenge, and invite us to rethink our surroundings and our impact on the world. It is a bold stride towards a future where the places we call home are a reflection of our collective commitment to more innovative, more empathetic, and more sustainable living.

Chapter 2

Advantages of Container Homes

Sustainability Factors

In the heart of modern architectural innovation, container homes emerge not just as a statement of style but as a deeply rooted answer to the clarion call for sustainability. This chapter delves into the profound environmental considerations that container homes address, sculpting a blueprint for a future where our homes are harmonized with the ethos of eco-conscious living.

The architectural landscape of our time is punctuated with challenges that stem from an increasing consciousness about the environment. It's no longer just about creating spaces that are visually stunning and functionally apt but about fostering environments that contribute to the health of our planet. In this context, container homes are more than a novelty; they are an embodiment of sustainable practice.

When an architect chooses a container home, they are engaging in an act of repurposing on a grand scale. These steel structures, initially designed for transporting goods across the oceans, find a second life as foundational elements of residential living spaces. The ecological footprint of manufacturing building materials is colossal. By reusing these containers, architects effectively divert the energy and raw materials that would have been consumed in constructing a similar space from scratch.

However, the sustainability factors of container homes extend beyond the mere reuse of materials. Their very nature compels a design philosophy that is inherently resource-efficient. The constraints of size and shape of containers encourage a minimalist approach, urging one to pare down to the essentials. This minimalist approach aligns with a broader understanding that smaller spaces, when well-designed, are not only adequate but desirable for sustainable living. They require less energy to heat and relax, less time to clean, and, ultimately, less material to maintain.

The insulative retrofitting of these homes further cements their sustainable status. By employing advanced insulation techniques, such as spray foam or panel insulation, a container home becomes a cocoon of energy efficiency, its metal walls transformed into barriers that keep the elements at bay, maintaining a comfortable interior climate with minimal energy input.

Moreover, the architectural flexibility that containers provide lends itself to a plethora of eco-friendly innovations. Green roofs, solar panels, and rainwater harvesting systems are not mere add-ons but integrate seamlessly with the container home ethos. A green roof atop a container not only insulates but also mitigates the heat island effect in urban settings, contributing to the remediation of one of the most pressing climatic issues in our concrete jungles.

The inherent durability of shipping containers also speaks volumes about their sustainability. Designed to withstand the rigors of sea travel, they are resistant to wind, water, and fire, outstripping many traditional building materials in terms of longevity. This resilience translates to lower maintenance requirements and a longer lifecycle, reducing the need for repair and renovation materials that tax our natural resources.

Sustainability is also reflected in the very process by which container homes come to life. The modular nature of container construction facilitates a significant portion of the work to be done off-site in controlled environments that minimize waste and maximize efficiency. This streamlined process not only cuts down on construction waste but also reduces the carbon emissions associated with traditional building practices.

As we contemplate the future of urban living, with its high-density populations and escalating environmental challenges, container homes stand out as bastions of sustainability. They challenge architects and residents alike to reconsider what it means to live well. To inhabit a container home is to make a powerful statement of intentionality, to live in a space that is both a personal sanctuary and a manifestation of one's commitment to a planet under duress.

In essence, the sustainability of container homes is not just a singular feature but a multi-faceted spectrum that touches upon every aspect of their existence—from conception to long-term habitation. For the environmentally attuned architect, they represent an opportunity to practice what they preach, to merge their professional expertise with their ethos, and to lead by example in the vital crusade for a more sustainable world.

Affordability and Time Efficiency

Imagine a home that not only underscores your commitment to the environment but also respects your need for economic sensibility and time management. The architecture of container homes embraces affordability and time efficiency, paramount virtues that are often elusive in traditional construction.

Amid the hustle of metropolitan life where every second and penny counts, container homes emerge as a solution that encapsulates both the urgency of time and the prudence of budget management. For the modern architect who juggles aesthetic zeal with financial acumen, container homes present an opportunity to revolutionize the way we think about building homes.

Affordability, the foremost advantage, is not just a byproduct of the container home phenomenon—it's the bedrock upon which it is built. Consider the economic landscape of urban living:

- Soaring real estate prices.

- The rising cost of construction materials.

- Labor charges that climb with complexity.

Now, juxtapose this with the cost-effectiveness of upcycling shipping containers, a resource already crafted and merely awaiting transformation. The economic argument for container homes becomes not just compelling but resoundingly clear.

These steel constructs, once retired from their voyages across the seas, are remarkably less expensive than conventional building materials. By repurposing them, architects tap into a reservoir of value, optimizing the lifecycle of the containers and minimizing the financial burden of material sourcing. This ingenuity in resource utilization reflects a profound shift in the economic underpinnings of home building.

However, affordability does not imply compromise. Container homes embody the essence of modernism—sleek, durable, and customizable to the zenith. Within their corrugated walls lies a canvas for architectural innovation, allowing for the creation of living spaces that rival, if not surpass, the allure of traditional homes. The difference, however, is the price point, which stands significantly lower, thus opening the doors of architectural elegance to a broader demographic.

Beyond cost, time efficiency is woven into the very fabric of container home construction. In a world where time is as valuable as currency, traditional building can be a protracted affair. Container homes, however, stride onto the scene with the promise of expedited construction timelines. The inherent modularity of shipping containers translates into a building block approach to construction, where much of the assembly is orchestrated with the precision and speed of a well-oiled machine.

The controlled environment of a container home workshop enables a significant portion of the build and fit-out to occur off-site. This parallel processing slashes months off the construction schedule, permitting a suitable transition from conception to habitation. In a fast-paced urban milieu, such agility is not just desirable but necessary.

This swift construction process is a testament to the synchrony between human ingenuity and the intrinsic properties of the containers. It is not simply about putting a structure together quickly; it is about redefining the process of making a house a home. With these timelines shortened, the architect finds themselves in a virtuous cycle, able to complete projects with greater frequency, hone their craft, and iterate designs with the dynamism that the modern housing market demands.

Additionally, time efficiency dovetails beautifully with the reduced environmental impact of container homes. Less time spent on-site equates to less energy consumed during the build phase, which cascades into a reduced carbon footprint. In this respect, time efficiency and sustainability are inextricably linked, each reinforcing the value of the other.

The synthesis of affordability and time efficiency in container homes is emblematic of a broader paradigm shift in architecture. It reflects a growing awareness that value-driven, rapid construction can coexist with architectural excellence. For the urban architect, this translates into a compelling offering for clients who seek the pinnacle of modern living—homes that are financially accessible, rapidly realized, and aesthetically captivating.

As we chart the course for future urban development, container homes stand at the vanguard, challenging us to rethink our approach to housing. They are a harbinger of an era where the dreams of homeownership align with the realities of economic and temporal constraints and where architects are the stewards of this transformative vision.

Flexibility and Modularity

In the architectural symphony of container homes, flexibility and modularity are the crescendos that have disrupted the concerto of traditional construction. The urban architect, a maestro of design and innovation, finds in container homes an instrument that responds adeptly to the delicate touch of creativity and the pressing demands of urbanization.

Flexibility is not merely an attribute; it's a philosophy that container homes embody. These steel ensembles once consigned to the monotony of carrying cargo, now aspire to a higher calling—morphing with the ease of a chameleon to fit the unique visions of dwellers and designers alike. This flexibility is the dance of possibility, where a single container can metamorphose into a cozy studio or, with the addition of its kind, a sprawling abode.

For the architect nestled in the heart of a bustling metropolis, space is at a premium, and the ability to customize is not just a luxury but a necessity. Container homes proffer a solution to this puzzle by offering an architectural grammar that is inherently flexible. Doors and windows may be etched into their Corten steel canvases with precision, while internal walls are as transient as the needs of the inhabitant.

Moreover, the flexibility extends to the heart of urban living. These structures can snugly fit into irregular urban lots, sometimes even perching themselves with ease in spaces that would rebuff the advances of traditional construction. They echo the modern individual's desire for a living space that is both an oasis and a chameleon—the ability to expand, contract, and evolve with life's stages.

Modularity, the kindred spirit of flexibility, is the cornerstone upon which the ethos of container homes is built. In the practice of architecture, where every constraint is a call for innovation, modularity offers a reprieve—a system that simplifies complexity. Container homes, with their modular nature, function much like the elemental building blocks of Lego, offering a plethora of combinations, each tailored to the desires of the dweller and the demands of the site.

The urban architect, accustomed to the constraints of rigid structures, finds liberation in this modularity. It permits the stacking and aligning of containers to forge homes that ascend toward the heavens or sprawl like a terrestrial constellation. This modularity is not just structural; it's a narrative of personal expression, where the layout of rooms and the interplay of spaces can be authored and re-authored over time.

From the perspective of architectural practice, the benefits are manifold. The modular aspect of container homes provides a reproducible yet customizable framework, enabling the architect to craft signature designs that can be replicated with variations across different projects. It is an opportunity to streamline and specialize, carving a niche in the competitive terrain of urban housing.

Furthermore, these homes, with their modularity, encourage a form of sustainable growth. As families grow and need change, so too can the home—without the wasteful and costly process of demolition and reconstruction. An additional room, an extra level, or a new wing can be integrated with minimal disruption, reflecting the organic evolution of human life.

The modular approach also streamlines the construction process itself, reducing on-site labor and the inherent unpredictability of traditional construction. It aligns with the architectural pursuit of efficiency, reducing the timelines and resources required to turn a concept into a habitable space.

In essence, the flexibility and modularity of container homes are a paradigm shift in urban housing. They afford the architect a medium that is at once steadfast and malleable, a paradox that catalyzes innovation. It is a renaissance in urban architecture, where the rigid boundaries of traditional construction give way to an era of dynamic, sustainable, and personalized living spaces.

As container homes rise in prominence within the urban fabric, they stand as testaments to the adaptability and ingenuity of modern architecture. They are not just structures but manifestations of the evolving ethos of urban life—flexible, modular, and infinitely adaptable to the pulsating rhythm of the city.

Chapter 3

Planning Your Container Home

Design Principles

In the heart of urban innovation, where steel intersects with the skyline and the demand for sustainability crescendos, the container home emerges as a symbol of architectural evolution. Here, we unfold the tapestry of design principles that guide the inception of a container home, drawing a fine line between avant-garde aesthetics and eco-conscious living.

The genesis of planning your container home begins with a profound respect for the environment. The dialogue between your home and its natural surroundings is intricate, informing every aspect from the strategic placement of fenestrations to the orientation of the entire structure. It's about capturing the sun's warmth, the breeze's coolness, and the land's contours to create a living space that is in harmony with its habitat. This principle ensures that the home maximizes the gifts of nature, using them to enhance livability while minimizing environmental impact.

In the realm of container homes, structural integrity transcends the mere capacity to withstand the elements—it's about reimagining a vessel built for the high seas into a steadfast sanctuary. The shipping container's innate durability is its boon, demanding a designer's eye to recalibrate its robustness for the permanence of land-based dwellings. This conversion process calls for a meticulous understanding of structural dynamics, ensuring that the container's resilience is uncompromised as it transforms into a home.

Spatial ingenuity is paramount in the compact quarters of a container. The challenge is to create a sense of openness within a predefined geometric expanse. The ingenious design transforms these rectangular volumes into a labyrinth of livability, maximizing utility while evoking an air of spaciousness. In this pursuit, the architect must employ a mélange of creativity and practicality, crafting multipurpose spaces that respond to both the immediate and the eventual needs of its occupants. This is where ingenuity shines—turning constraints into catalysts for innovation.

The aesthetic identity of a container home is forged from the alchemy of raw industrialism and personalized style. The architect's palette must blend the container's corrugated steel charm with elements that speak to the individuality of the homeowner. This interplay of materials, textures, and hues requires a nuanced balance—enhancing rather than overpowering the container's character. The resulting aesthetic should not only captivate the eye but also evoke a sense of belonging.

Utility and fluidity go hand in hand as cornerstones of functional design. A container home should be as adaptive as it is comfortable, embracing the fluidity of modern life where change is the only constant. Designing for versatility means anticipating the evolution of the home's life cycle—from a bachelor's haven to a family abode, from a workspace to a retreat. This principle implores the designer to envision a home that evolves, spaces that reconfigure, and a layout that accommodates the shifting sands of time.

Sustainability is the keystone in the arch of container home design. It is present in the conscious selection of materials that insulate, systems that conserve, and layouts that reduce the ecological footprint of the home. Each choice, from renewable energy sources to sustainable water systems, intertwines to create a habitat that exemplifies responsible living. The container home becomes a manifesto of sustainability, championing a lifestyle that honors the earth while showcasing the pinnacle of green technology and design.

The final stroke in the planning phase is ensuring that the container home does not exist in isolation but is a harmonious extension of its urban tapestry. This contextual cohesion involves understanding the neighborhood's architectural vernacular and reflecting it in the container home without compromising its distinctiveness. It's about creating a home that resonates with its environment, complements its surroundings, and yet stands out as a testament to innovative design.

In crafting a container home, these principles guide the architect's hand, marrying vision with responsibility and innovation with reverence for the planet. The journey from concept to creation is a delicate balance of artistry, ingenuity, and environmental stewardship. As the blueprint unfolds, let these principles illuminate the path to a home that is not merely a structure but a living, breathing extension of human ingenuity and nature's bounty. This container home stands as a beacon of sustainable and innovative architecture in the ever-evolving urban landscape.

Site Selection and Assessment

Choosing the perfect site for your container home is akin to an artist selecting a canvas. It is the ground upon which your vision will take form, where your sustainable dreams will root, and where your architectural passions will manifest into reality. As an architect in the crescendo of your career, this choice becomes the cornerstone of innovation, sustainability, and personal statement in the urban tapestry you inhabit.

In the search for the ideal site, consider the narrative you want your container home to tell. Is it one of urban retreats, a harmonious blend with nature, or a defiant statement of modernity against the city's skyline? Each plot of land holds a unique profile—its topography, its relationship to the sun and wind, and its connectivity to the pulse of city life.

Assessing a site begins with the lie of the land. The topography dictates the design possibilities, challenges, and potential for integration with the container's inherently linear form. A sloped site might offer panoramic views and opportunities for multi-level designs that play with gravity, but it also demands rigorous structural calculations and, possibly, more complex foundations. On the contrary, a flat parcel of land offers ease of construction but might necessitate inventive design to elevate its character.

Sunlight is the artist's best medium, and in container home design, it serves a dual purpose—esthetic illumination and energy efficiency. Study the sun's path across your prospective site to determine how to capture its warmth, create light-filled spaces, and where to place solar panels for optimal energy capture. This dance with the sun is a delicate balance between harnessing its power and mitigating its intensity through intelligent design and orientation.

The whisper of the wind through your home can either be a cooling caress or a howling challenge. Understanding the prevalent wind patterns is crucial for natural ventilation, a component that is inherently sustainable and will dictate the placement of windows and terraces. It's an opportunity to let the environment shape your living space, allowing you to design with the climate rather than against it.

Connectivity in an urban setting is pivotal. Your site should not only reflect your ethos of sustainable living but also connect seamlessly with the amenities and arteries of city life. An ideal site would offer sanctuary from the urban rush while still keeping the city's conveniences within reach. This balancing act is crucial in selecting a site that fulfills both personal and professional life requirements.

With the principles of sustainability etched into your ethos, evaluating the environmental impact of your container home starts from the ground up. The site should offer the potential for rainwater harvesting, minimal disruption to the local ecology, and the ability to integrate green spaces, edible gardens, or even permaculture principles.

Assessment extends beyond the physical to the bureaucratic landscape. The urban architect must navigate the labyrinth of zoning regulations, building codes, and permit requirements—a prelude to the design process. It requires due diligence to ensure that the chosen site will not encounter legal impediments that may hinder construction or future expansion.

And then, there's the soul of the site—something not found in topographic maps or zoning documents. It's the intangible essence that resonates with your vision of home. It's the morning mist that rolls over the land, the way the city lights flicker at dusk, the serene hush that blankets the space—these are the nuances that make a location more than a site; they are what make it a foundation for your container home.

Your choice of a site is a reflection of your values, an embodiment of your design principles, and a statement of your architectural legacy. It is where your journey into the niche of container home architecture takes root, where your sustainable dreams intersect with reality, and where your personal and professional aspirations coalesce into the tangible form of innovative, minimalist living.

In the symphony of site selection and assessment, let each consideration be a note that contributes to the harmony of your container home's existence—a melody that plays to the rhythm of the city, the serenity of nature, and the ethos of an architect who values sustainability as much as the shelter itself.

Obtaining Necessary Permits

The journey from conception to reality for a container home involves an encounter with the often-daunting world of permits and regulations. For you, the passionate architect, it's an opportunity to bring your innovative vision within the lines of legal frameworks, ensuring that your sustainable creation stands not only as a testament to green living but also to the art of navigating bureaucracy with intelligence and foresight.

The intricate dance with permits begins with an understanding of what's required. Each city and each neighborhood can have its labyrinthine set of codes, each a riddle to be solved. Start with zoning permits—these are the keys to unlocking your project. Zoning permits confirm that your land is used for residential purposes and that your container home aligns with local development plans. It's a check against the future, ensuring your home fits within the grand scheme of urban growth.

Building permits, the cornerstone of construction legality, ensure that your design is scrutinized against safety standards, building codes, and structural requirements. It's the green light that says your blueprints can move from paper to the physical, from ideas to beams and bolts. Engaging with building inspectors is not a hurdle but a partnership, a collective effort to ensure the structure you conceive is safe for occupation and enduring against the elements.

The permit process extends its tendrils into the specifics of home construction—electrical permits, plumbing permits, and, in some cases, mechanical permits. This granular level of approval is a check against the risk, a safeguard for those who will dwell within the container walls. Each inspection and each approval are a stamp of reliability, a nod to the foresight in your planning.

For the container home, unusual by the standards of traditional housing, obtaining permits can also mean education. You are not merely an architect; you become an advocate, introducing officials to the robust safety, sustainability, and suitability of shipping containers as living spaces. Your permit applications are not just requests; they're presentations, a showcase of innovation that must win the confidence of those more accustomed to concrete and wood than corrugated steel.

Utility permits ensure your container home is connected to the lifeblood of urban living—water, electricity, and sewage. It's here that your sustainable principles face the test, weaving in rainwater harvesting systems, solar arrays, or composting toilets into the fabric of municipal services, showing that living off-grid or with a minimal footprint can dovetail with the grid's edge.

In securing permits, expect a journey through revisions and appeals. Rarely does a unique project like a container home pass through the gauntlet without challenge. View each question and each request for clarification as a step toward a better, more robust design. It's a dialogue, sometimes taxing, often enlightening, but always aimed at refinement.

During this phase, you embody the architect as both creator and communicator. You'll translate the technical into the tangible for permit officers, sometimes demystifying the details of a design that may first appear foreign to their eyes. Your dialogue with the permitting authorities becomes as much about education as it is about compliance, forging a path for future architects to follow in your innovative footsteps.

And remember, patience here is more than a virtue; it's a strategic asset. The time taken to secure permits should not be seen as lost but rather as invested—ensuring the longevity and legality of your container home. It's the bureaucratic groundwork that anchors your sustainable ambitions firmly in reality.

As you navigate the red tape, keep your vision in clear sight. Each form, each submission, and each day spent in the permit office is a step toward materializing the eco-friendly dwelling that may very well become a beacon in your architectural career and a signature of your personal belief in sustainability.

When the final permit is secured, the effort invested becomes part of the home's story—a narrative of dedication, of a willingness to bridge the gap between the avant-garde and the established, and of the triumph of an architect who not only designs but also perseveres. Your container home, then, is not just a structure; it's a testament to the passion and persistence that define both your craft and your contribution to the urban fabric.

Chapter 4

Designing Your Container Home

Architectural Design Basics

The voyage into the architectural design of a container home is as much an exploration of innovation as it is a return to the roots of sustainability and minimalism. For the architect who values the blend of utility and aesthetics, the container home is a unique canvas—one that promises a marriage of form and function within the bounds of repurposed industrial charm and modern comfort.

In the realm of container home design, we begin by acknowledging the industrial genesis of our primary material: the shipping container. It is a structural unit that speaks a language of durability and simplicity. This language informs the basis of our design, urging us to maintain the integrity of the container's shape while simultaneously invoking a new purpose. Your design must encapsulate the container's essence—its linearity, uniformity, and modularity—while transforming its steel composition into a living, breathing home.

When we speak of architecture, we talk of shaping environments that cater to the human experience. The design of a container home must pivot on how its inhabitants will interact with the space. The morning light filtering through a living area, the ease of movement through a kitchen, the privacy afforded in a bedroom—all these experiences are premeditated in your design blueprint. The home becomes a theatre for life's daily rituals, where the industrial meets the domestic, not in a collision, but in a dance of coexistence.

Designing with adaptability in mind ensures the home can evolve alongside the changing lives of those it shelters. The spaces must be envisioned to accommodate growth and change—a studio transforming into a nursery, a reading nook becoming an at-home workspace. This adaptive design is your commitment to the future, ensuring that the home can mature as gracefully as its inhabitants with minimal structural upheaval.

Beyond the adaptability of spaces, your design must incorporate the technical aspects—mechanical, electrical, and plumbing systems—with a finesse that hides their complexity within the simplicity of the design. The actual architectural challenge lies in embedding these systems so seamlessly that their presence is a discreet whisper, one that supports the lives of those within without compromising the integrity of the design.

Your design tells a story—a narrative of transformation from a life of transit across oceans to one firmly rooted in the domestic landscape. Each element of the design speaks to this journey, balancing the raw, industrial aesthetic with elements that soften and humanize. The container's corrugated walls, the echoes of its past life, remain visible, yet they now frame views of the outdoors, hold shelves of books, or encase cozy spaces for sleep and solitude.

The fundamentals of architectural design in the context of container homes are rooted in a set of core values:

- Sustainability is embedded in the very act of repurposing.

- Simplicity is echoed in the unadorned elegance of the container's form.

- Strength is inherent in the steel construction and in the home's ability to withstand the test of time.

With each design decision, you are not just constructing spaces but advocating a set of ideals, casting a vision for a future where architecture eschews excess in favor of essence.

In your role as an architect, you are tasked not just with creating a structure but with instilling a soul within the steel. The container home stands as a physical manifestation of innovative design thinking, a space that is at once a sanctuary and a statement. It is a reflection of the modern desire to live less encumbered, more connected to our environments, and more aware of our impact on the world.

Your container home design, therefore, becomes a microcosm of architectural philosophy, challenging the conventions of traditional housing and redefining the essence of home. It is not merely a place of residence but a living, evolving testament to what architecture can achieve when ingenuity partners with intentionality.

In conclusion, the architectural design basics of container homes call for a profound understanding of the material's origins, an empathy towards the end-user's experiences, and an innovative spirit that dares to redefine the norms of living spaces. Your blueprint, drawn from these principles, will not just lay the foundation for a home but will pave the way for a new chapter in sustainable living, echoing the voices of minimalism, durability, and environmental consciousness for generations to come.

Optimizing for Energy Efficiency

Nestled within the innovative frontier of sustainable architecture, the allure of a shipping container home is not solely in its eco-friendly repurposement or its striking industrial aesthetic; it is also in its potential for unparalleled energy efficiency. In the pursuit of an eco-conscious existence, optimizing a container home for energy efficiency is both an art and a science—a symphony of design elements that resonate with the rhythms of nature and the latest advancements in green technology.

At the heart of this optimization is the intimate understanding of the shipping container's material virtues and limitations. These steel behemoths, once braving the high seas, are inherently conductive, a characteristic that poses a challenge in maintaining internal temperature without thoughtful modification. Thus, the transformative journey from a cold metal shell to an energy-efficient abode is underpinned by meticulous planning and innovation.

The design starts with orientation—the positioning of your container home is a critical first note that sets the tempo for energy conservation. A thoughtful orientation takes advantage of the sun's trajectory, embracing its warmth in the cooler months while shielding against its oppressive heat when summer arrives. Such strategic placement is the prelude to an energy-efficient design, leveraging natural light and warmth, reducing reliance on artificial heating and lighting, and thus, curtailing energy consumption.

Insulation is the melody to this symphony—an absolute essential that serves as the barrier between the harshness of external elements and the comfort of your interior spaces. Spray foam insulation can be likened to a virtuoso performance, filling every nook with a protective layer that keeps heat in during winter and out during summer. This choice not only optimizes thermal performance but also contributes to sound dampening, turning the once-booming echo of a steel container into a serene whisper.

Windows and doors are the crescendo, pivotal in energy optimization. Selecting high-quality, double-paned glass can significantly reduce energy loss, akin to placing the perfect acoustic panels in a concert hall. The positioning of these elements requires a careful composition—maximizing natural light while minimizing heat gain, achieving a delicate balance that is as much about aesthetic harmony as it is about energy efficiency.

Within these steel walls, energy-efficient appliances hum in quiet efficiency, selected for their low power draw and high performance. LED lighting, energy-rated refrigerators, and efficient water heaters are the unsung heroes in the daily life of a container home, each contributing to a lower energy score and a lighter ecological footprint.

The roof, often an overlooked character in the energy narrative, offers a space of potential. With the addition of solar panels, it becomes a dynamic surface that captures the sun's energy, transforming your home into a power-generating vessel. A living roof, planted with vegetation, can insulate and cool, transforming a once lifeless expanse into a thriving ecosystem.

Heating and cooling systems, the virtuoso soloists, demand careful selection. Options such as mini-split systems, which offer zoned climate control, become the cornerstone of an energy-efficient temperature regulation strategy. These systems provide on-demand comfort with minimal energy input, celebrating efficiency with each whisper-quiet cycle.

Even the colors chosen for your container home play their part in this energy opus. Light hues reflect the sun's rays, reducing the need for air conditioning, while darker tones absorb heat, a boon in chillier climes.

An energy-efficient container home is not merely a shelter but a living testament to sustainable innovation. Each design decision and each technological integration is a deliberate step towards reducing the carbon footprint, living in harmony with the environment, and setting a precedent in modern, minimalist living. This approach to design is not just about saving on bills or adhering to trends—it is about crafting spaces that sustain our resources and nourish the soul.

In this era of heightened environmental consciousness, optimizing for energy efficiency transcends mere utility; it reflects a more profound ethos and a responsibility towards the planet and future generations. As architects, we wield the power to shape not just structures but also the trajectory of our collective environmental impact. And so, as we draw the blueprints for our container homes, we are not just outlining walls and windows; we are charting a course for a cleaner, greener, and more efficient way of life.

Customization Ideas

The modern architect, standing on the threshold of innovation and sustainability, finds a canvas for creative expression in the humble shipping container. As the heartbeats of global trade are repurposed into homes, they embody a new paradigm of living space. The customization of a container home is not just an exercise in design; it is a statement of personality, a manifesto of minimalism, and a commitment to the environment.

Customization in container home design is about breaking free from the traditional confines of architecture. The rigid geometry of the container is a challenge to the creative mind, a puzzle that begs for a unique solution. It asks for a vision that sees beyond the corrugated steel walls and envisions a living space that is both a refuge and a work of art.

Let's unfold this tapestry of customization where each thread is a unique idea brought to life by the designer's touch. Customization begins with the container itself. Standard sizes provide a starting point, but the modular nature of these steel units allows for a variety of configurations. By stacking, cutting, and rearranging, one can sculpt a space that is as open or as intimate as desired. Imagine a home where walls slide away to reveal expanses of glass, blurring the lines between indoors and out, where roof terraces capitalize on urban views, and sunken living rooms offer an unexpected twist to the interior landscape.

In these spaces, doors, and windows are not mere portals but are elements of surprise and ingenuity. A garage-style roll-up door transforms a living room into an open-air lounge, inviting the cityscape or serene countryside inside. Skylights puncture ceilings, allowing daylight to cascade through the home, while custom cut-outs in the container walls create picture frames for the world outside.

Interior finishes are where the individual's touch becomes most apparent. In a world where every surface can be customized, the walls of a container home become a gallery. Wood cladding warms the industrial edges, while exposed metal accents pay homage to the container's origins. Polished concrete floors lay a foundation of urban chic, as reclaimed materials tell a story of sustainability and texture.

The heartbeat of customization is in the details. Custom-built furniture that folds, slides, and hides away can transform a space from an office to a bedroom, a dining area to a lounge with effortless grace. Built-in bookshelves, dropdown desks, and convertible pieces are not just furniture; they are functional sculptures that define the living space.

In the kitchen, customization offers a symphony of efficiency and style. Compact appliances, reflective of a conscientious lifestyle, nestle into countertops of recycled glass or repurposed wood. At the same time, storage solutions echo the minimalist ethos with a place for everything and everything in its place.

Bathrooms in container homes can be realms of indulgence or models of efficiency. Customization here might mean a Japanese soaking tub set against a backdrop of lush green walls, a nod to the tiny house movement's ingenious use of space and the growing trend of biophilic design.

Technology, too, plays its part in this custom design concerto. Smart home systems that manage lighting, climate, and security weave convenience and efficiency into the fabric of the home. These systems offer not just the ease of automation but also a way to monitor and minimize energy usage, a testament to the home's sustainable heart.

Outdoor spaces are as much a part of the home as the interior. Decks and patios extend the living area, and with customization, they become oases in the sky or secret gardens. A rooftop deck, accessible by a custom-designed spiral staircase, brings the vastness of the sky to the urban dweller. At the same time, a patio edged with container planters offers a private retreat in the midst of the city's bustle.

In the end, the customization of a container home is about crafting a space that reflects the soul of its inhabitants. It's a process of making choices that resonate with one's values and aesthetics. The container home becomes a personal manifesto, a living, breathing space that not only houses the body but also nurtures the spirit.

For the architect who sees beyond the constraints of four walls, a container home is a dream of form and function. It's a space where the rhythms of city life meet the quiet of solitude, where the industrial becomes intimate, and where the home is not just built but is created. This is the art of customization in container homes, where each decision, each design, is an echo of the individual and a vision for a sustainable future.

Chapter 5

Acquiring Shipping Containers

Where to Find Containers

In the architect's grand design, the act of sourcing the core elements—shipping containers—becomes a foundational chapter in the narrative of creating a sustainable home. Each container is a capsule of possibility, a promise of transformation from a practical steel box to a living, breathing space. The task of finding these containers is not a mere acquisition; it is an integral part of the creative process, a reflection of the architect's commitment to sustainability and innovation.

Starting the journey at the ports, where the air is thick with the scent of sea and metal, one can find the genesis of many a container's story. The shipping yards serve as a repository for these structures that have crossed oceans, each dent and scratch a testament to their global journey. One-trip containers stand in the ranks, too, nearly pristine, ready for a less turbulent second life. They are more than steel—they are the raw canvas upon which the architect's vision will be rendered.

Yet, ports are not the sole haven for these steel marvels. The urban fabric is interwoven with dealers and resellers, professionals who have turned the rehoming of containers into their craft. They offer a variety of conditions, from the untouched to those pre-modified, perhaps with a window cut here or an insulation layer added there. Engaging with these intermediaries can ease logistical burdens, often bringing with them services that deliver right to your building site, introducing a convenience that is well suited for the busy metropolitan professional.

The digital realm has expanded the horizon for container hunters, with online marketplaces boasting a vast and ever-shifting inventory of available units. Here, one can sift through countless options with precision, comparing prices and conditions, often stumbling upon listings that offer a local pick-up option, thus reducing the carbon footprint of transportation. The hunt can be clinical, yes, but also surprisingly intimate as one uncovers the right fit amongst the digital noise.

In contrast to the bustling world of commerce, government and military surplus auctions offer a more systematic approach to procurement. Containers here may come with a story of service, having once sheltered supplies or equipment in far-flung locales. They require a prepared and decisive architect, one ready to navigate the unique rhythms of the auction world where the gavel's fall signifies a new beginning for these retired containers.

The relationships an architect forges can also lead to sources less traveled. Local storage companies often rotate their inventory, selling older models to make way for the new. These conversations can foster a community connection, potentially opening doors to ongoing sources as the company continues to refresh its stock.

Venturing into rural expanses, one may find containers that have been repurposed as storage for agricultural tools or produce. These finds often require refurbishment but come with the benefit of a lower price and the potential for a rustic charm that only history can bestow.

There's also the path of direct communication with shipping lines. By engaging in dialogue with these companies, an architect may not only secure a container but also establish a partnership that could facilitate a steady supply for future projects, ensuring a consistent aesthetic or quality for the practice.

Amidst these traditional avenues, there is a rising tide of global repurposing initiatives—groups dedicated to finding sustainable solutions for decommissioned shipping containers. Aligning with such initiatives resonates with the architect's philosophy, where each material chosen is an active vote for a future where re-use is not just aesthetic but ethical.

In the pursuit of these steel shells, the architect embraces roles as varied as the investigator, the negotiator, and the visionary. It's a journey that requires a blend of persistence, insight, and foresight. Each container carries with it a life lived, and it is up to the architect to write its next chapter. The resulting home will not merely be a structure of convenience but a statement, a testament to a belief in reclamation and innovation.

The search for shipping containers, then, is more than a mere step in the construction process. It is a reflection of the architect's ethos, a tangible expression of commitment to crafting spaces that not only house lives but also tell tales of global journeys, past purposes, and sustainable futures. As the architect selects each container, they are not just choosing a unit of space—they are curating a legacy of resourcefulness, aesthetics, and responsibility that will stand as the cornerstone of their sustainable architectural practice.

Selecting the Right Type

Embarking on the path of creating a container home is akin to that of an artist facing a selection of canvases, each with distinct textures, sizes, and potentials. The architect stands before an array of steel monoliths, each with a unique story to tell, each offering a different promise of home. These containers, the building blocks of a modern, minimalist sanctuary, are not just selected; they are understood and envisioned in their new life as part of a sustainable abode.

As an architect, imagine standing in a vast container depot, where the air hums with the echoes of global travel and the ground vibrates with the weight of history.

Here, amidst rows of corrugated steel, you find the standard 20-foot containers, the stalwarts of the industry, offering a compact living space that challenges the occupant to embrace minimalism and ingenuity. Their larger counterparts, the 40-foot containers, stand proud, promising a more generous breadth for design and living.

But the decision extends beyond mere dimensions. High-cube containers beckon those who dream of high ceilings and airy spaces. In contrast, specialized "open-top" or "open-side" containers present a canvas for those who dare to infuse their designs with the natural world, blurring the lines between inside and outside. The material of these containers—predominantly Corten steel known for its weathering properties or the lighter aluminum—carries implications for the home's durability and environmental impact.

Beyond the physical attributes, an architect's selection is influenced by the life story of each container. One-trip containers stand almost new, pristine, and ready, yet they carry a higher cost—financial and environmental. In contrast, the veterans of the sea, with their dents and rusted patinas, speak of resilience and a life well-traveled. These used containers carry a narrative, a character that will permeate through the walls of a future home.

The narrative continues as the architect considers the container's past purposes—whether it has insulated walls as a refrigerated unit or bore loads of dry goods. Each history presents unique challenges and opportunities for repurposing into a habitable space. When envisioning the modifications necessary to transform these steel boxes into living spaces, the inherent structural integrity and the extent of the interventions become a critical part of the selection process.

Furthermore, the correct type of container is also one that harmonizes with the regulatory symphony of building codes and zoning laws. These are the unseen boundaries within which a container home must be sculpted, and they cannot be ignored. Each type, size, and material bring its own set of constraints and freedoms in this dance of compliance.

Energy efficiency is another guiding star in the selection process. The orientation of the container, the surface area for potential solar panel installation, and the opportunities for natural insulation are all determined by the type of container chosen. A container's suitability for a green home is not just in its ability to be recycled into a living space but also in how it can sustain and support the lives within through energy-conscious design.

In the domain of acoustics, the selection is finely tuned. Steel containers may challenge the serenity of a home with their propensity to echo, yet with foresight, they can be transformed into a cocoon of serenity through meticulous planning and design—again impacting the choice of container.

Ultimately, the longevity and resilience of the home hinge on this selection. While Corten steel promises decades of endurance with proper care, an aluminum container, though less enduring, offers a testament to the architect's commitment to a lighter environmental footprint.

In crafting a container home, the act of selecting the right type is less of a choice and more of a partnership with the material. It is an intimate dance between the architect's vision and the container's inherent qualities. The final choice is a commitment, not just to a style or a statement but to a journey of sustainable, innovative living. This journey will culminate in a space that is not just constructed but conscientiously brought to life, a testament to the architect's vision and a sanctuary that stands as an emblem of modern, sustainable living.

Transportation and Delivery

In the creative symphony that is the construction of a container home, the movement of the steel ensemble from the container depot to the building site is a passage filled with meticulous orchestration. The transportation and delivery of these colossal building blocks require not just logistical planning but an intuitive understanding of urban spaces, a commitment to sustainability, and a foresight into the unfolding narrative of modern habitat.

Envision the journey: shipping containers, the once silent giants of international trade, are repurposed to become the core of a pioneering architectural venture. Each container's odyssey, from a practical object to a bespoke element of someone's abode, is as unique as the design it will soon embody. This process is not merely transactional; it's transformational.

The urban architect, our reader, knows the streets of the city like the lines on their blueprints. The challenge, then, is to maneuver these containers through the vibrant veins of the metropolis. Transportation methods are not selected; they are designed, taking into consideration the width of roads, the height of overpasses, the weight restrictions of bridges, and the chorus of city traffic. These factors dictate whether the container will journey on a flatbed, escorted by the flash of hazard lights, or require the delicate ballet of a crane in tighter spaces.

Delivery is a critical scene in this narrative. Timing is everything. It is about ensuring that the containers arrive as the site is prepared to welcome them to avoid any unnecessary dwell time that would not only disrupt the urban flow but also add to the environmental footprint of the project. The architect considers the season, the ebb and flow of urban life, and the silent hours of dawn when the city's pulse is low, and the arrival of a container can be as soft as the morning light.

Upon arrival, the container's placement is a dance of precision. Each container must descend on the prepared foundations with grace, aligning with predetermined markings that ensure the vision of the home remains undisturbed. This is where the architect's role transcends the norm, becoming not just a designer of spaces but a choreographer of heavy material, a conductor of steel and space.

The chosen transportation company is not just a service provider but a partner in the architect's commitment to sustainability. Their practices, their carbon footprint, the efficiency of their routes, and the cleanliness of their fleet are reflections of the home's ethos. It is a collaborative effort to ensure that the environmental impact of the container's movement is minimized and that every mile traveled does not weigh heavily upon the conscience of those who will dwell within the container walls.

Furthermore, the architect must navigate the often-complex terrain of permits and regulations. Each municipality sings its opera of rules, and each street has its tempo of allowance. Securing the correct permits for transportation is as essential as any other aspect of the building. It requires an understanding of local laws, a relationship with community officials, and, often, a touch of patience and negotiation.

Let's consider an example that weaves these threads together. A 40-foot container, selected for its noble dimensions and one-trip cleanliness, requires delivery to a site nestled in the historic heart of a bustling city. The architect must consider the route—avoiding the morning market streets and coordinating with the transit authorities for a late-night delivery. A specialized low-emission hauler is contracted, one with the capability to navigate narrow lanes. Upon reaching the destination, a local crane operator, familiar with the city's rhythm, lifts and places the container with the precision of a practiced hand.

The transportation and delivery of shipping containers are as much about the journey as the destination. It is about understanding that each mile traversed is a step closer to realizing a dream, a vision of a sustainable, innovative home. It is a process that demands respect for the urban tapestry, a commitment to the environment, and a deep engagement with the tactile, dynamic process of creating something extraordinary from the ordinary. For the architect, it is another beautiful layer in the rich experience of bringing a container home from concept to reality, a chapter that underscores the adventure of creation.

Chapter 6

Preparing the Building Site

Site Clearing and Preparation

For an architect whose craft is an extension of their identity, the initiation of site clearing and preparation is the moment where the concept becomes tangible. It is the blank canvas upon which the sustainable ethos of shipping container homes is grounded, a prelude to architectural innovation. Each motion in this phase is an articulation of respect for the land and the embodiment of a minimalist philosophy that finds beauty in simplicity and strength in restraint.

Before any soil is turned, the preparation phase begins with a thorough site assessment. Understanding the ecosystem that will cradle the container home is fundamental. It is a process that marries the precision of science with the intuition of artistry. The topography whispers its constraints and opportunities, the native vegetation gestures toward the sun's path, and the local fauna hint at the rhythms of the land. An architect's hand must be guided not only by the compass and level but also by an inherent stewardship of the environment.

The act of clearing is undertaken with a scalpel's precision rather than a bulldozer's brute force. It is the selective editing of the landscape to preserve as much of the natural context as possible. This meticulous approach aligns with the sustainable core of container homes, each decision weighted by its environmental impact. Careful excavation ensures that the natural drainage patterns of the site are not disrupted. Soil is respected, not simply removed, held aside to be reincorporated to maintain the site's integrity and minimize erosion.

In an urban setting, where the metropolitan hum and the scarcity of space challenge the conventional, the clearing might require the gentle negotiation of existing structures, a testament to the architect's commitment to resourcefulness and regeneration. It's about extracting value from every square inch, ensuring the land's history is not erased but rather integrated into the new narrative.

The setting of boundaries is not an act of division but the foundational gesture of creation. Stakes and strings delineate the future home's footprint, the first sketch of the structure to come. It is an outline that not only frames the work ahead but also symbolizes the commitment to precision that is the architect's signature. The surveyor's markers become a geometric ballet, setting the stage for the foundation and ensuring that the container's placement will be a perfect union of design and space.

Grading the site then becomes a sculptural process, a deliberate and thoughtful transformation that sets the tone for the entire project. The architect considers not just the immediate effect of this landscaping but how rainwater will navigate the property, how the ground will embrace the foundation, and how the home will settle into its surroundings. Each contour crafted in the earth is a future echo of the container home's lines, a preparation that holds both aesthetic and functional significance.

As the clearing concludes and the site begins to reveal the form of the future home, it becomes a tangible expression of the architect's vision. The once unmarked land now holds the intention of sustainable living, the foundation upon which a minimalist masterpiece will rise. This preparation is a declaration of principles, a clear demonstration that the home to be created here is not an imposition on the landscape but a harmonious extension of it.

In this context, an example is more than illustrative; it is a reflection of the architect's ethos. A plot of land within an urban renewal zone is chosen, its earth compacted by the memory of structures past. The clearing process must navigate around an ancient oak, a silent sentinel whose presence will become a focal point of the home's design. The preparation embraces the tree, incorporating it into the container home's lifeblood, its branches destined to play with the light and shadows of the structure's steel walls.

Thus, site clearing and preparation are stages of profound importance in the creation of a container home. It is a deliberate, intentional act that respects the past, honors the present, and anticipates the future. For the architect, it is a ritual that reaffirms their role not just as a builder of homes but as a curator of environments, a protector of ecosystems, and a pioneer of sustainable innovation. It is where the vision takes root, setting the stage for a home that embodies the ideals of minimalism, functionality, and harmony with the environment.

Foundation Types for Container Homes

In the pursuit of erecting a container home, an architect must make a profound decision that lays the groundwork for the future: choosing the appropriate foundation. This choice is not a mere technicality—it is a profound statement of intent, a commitment to a sustainable and minimalist lifestyle, and a thoughtful response to the challenges and opportunities presented by urban living. The foundation is the quiet custodian of a home's stability. For container homes, it is also an essential emblem of the architect's vision, resonating with the rhythms of city life while answering the calls of ecological sensitivity.

Consider the pier foundation—a series of strategic supports acting as an intermediary between the home and the earth. It is like acupuncture for the land, minimalistic in approach but significant in impact. The pier foundation is ideal for urban sites where the integrity of existing infrastructure is paramount. Each pier is carefully positioned to harmonize with the environment, minimizing the disturbance to the land while creating a sturdy base for the container home.

Transitioning to the slab foundation, we encounter a different philosophy—one of uniformity and solidarity. In the city's heart, where every square foot is a premium, the slab becomes a canvas of concrete, a declaration of permanence. It forms a steadfast base for the container home, providing a durable and reliable platform for construction and, equally important, for life itself.

The strip foundation takes a more nuanced approach. This continuous band of concrete embraces the container home's perimeter, providing a stable ledge while respecting the land's contours. It adapts to the urban lot with precision, ensuring the home is anchored securely. Yet, it does so with a sensitivity that allows the architecture to respond to the particularities of its site—a reclaimed parcel of the city, perhaps, where past and future converge.

For plots where the earth beneath is less than reliable, pile foundations offer a persistent solution. They reach deep, past the superficial layers of the ground, to grasp at the underlying stability. In an urban setting where other structures might shy away, a pile foundation allows the container home to assert its presence confidently, embracing the challenge of a demanding environment and turning it into a bastion of tranquility amid the urban tumult.

The architect's role in selecting a foundation transcends the act of building; it is a profound exercise in establishing harmony between the home and its urban context. It is the first indelible mark made on the site—a mark that speaks volumes about the home's relationship with its surroundings and its occupants' values.

A pier foundation engages with the site with respect and care, each pier a testament to thoughtful impact. A slab foundation is a steadfast commitment, a solid affirmation of a home's place within the urban tapestry. A strip foundation, meanwhile, traces the land's form with grace and agility, offering a solid edge for the home's upward trajectory. And a pile foundation, deep and steadfast, promises security and steadfastness in a city that never sleeps.

Ultimately, the foundation is the bedrock upon which the container home's story is built. It is the unseen strength that holds the home upright against the elements and the pressures of urban life. The proper foundation turns a collection of repurposed containers into a sanctuary, a personal haven that stands as a testament to innovative, sustainable living in the concrete jungle.

In summary, the choice of foundation for a container home is a critical first step that demands careful consideration. Whether one opts for the punctual precision of piers, the unwavering uniformity of a slab, the adaptable assurance of a strip, or the deep dedication of piles, the foundation not only supports the structure but also lays the groundwork for a home that embodies the architectural ethos of sustainability, minimalism, and profound respect for the urban environment. It is the silent statement, the invisible innovation, that distinguishes a mere dwelling from a home with a soul.

Chapter 7

Modifying Your Containers

Cutting and Framing Techniques

In the heart of every shipping container lies the potential for transformation, a metamorphosis guided by the hands of the architect who, like an alchemist, turns steel into living space. The process of cutting and framing is the critical stage where vision meets reality, where the rigid geometry of a cargo container evolves into the soft contours of a home.

To pierce the skin of a container is to embark on a journey of precision and caution, of knowing not only where to cut but how to cut. Each incision is a deliberate stroke, removing parts of the steel to create windows to the soul of the future dwelling and doorways to invite life inside. It's a meticulous dance with the material—too much force, and the structure protests; too little, and the vision remains trapped in a steel cocoon.

The tools of this craft are chosen for their precision and reliability. Plasma cutters, grinders, and cutting torches become extensions of the architect's intent, each slice of the blade a deliberate mark in the transformation process. The plasma cutter, with its high-velocity jet of ionized gas, makes quick work of the corrugated steel, while the grinding wheel smooths the edges to a soft finish, ensuring that the roughness of the sea's journey is left behind.

Once the cutting is complete, framing begins. It is here that the skeleton of the home takes shape, a lattice of reinforcement that speaks to both necessity and aesthetics. The steel frame that is erected within the container's shell serves multiple purposes—it compensates for the removed material, ensuring structural integrity, and forms the skeleton upon which interior walls and ceilings will hang.

The framing process often uses recycled steel or sustainable timber, adhering to the ethos of minimalism and sustainability. The architect chooses materials not only for their strength but for their story—each beam supports a narrative thread in the tapestry of the home's life. Steel beams are welded into place, their joints a permanent bond, while timber frames are measured and cut, then secured with the precision that speaks of a deeper understanding of materials.

In urban spaces, where the melody of life plays a complex key, the modifications to containers must respect the symphony of the surroundings. Windows cut into the steel bring in light, but not just any light—the light that complements the internal space and harmonizes with the city's rhythm. Frames for glass and insulating materials are then carefully installed, ensuring that the home's inhabitants remain connected to the urban scape while nestled in their sanctuaries.

The cutting and framing techniques are thus not merely about altering the form of a container but about understanding its future role. It is an exercise in balance—maintaining structural integrity while creating spaces that breathe and that live. The cuts map the home's function—living areas, kitchens, baths—each defined by the architect's intelligent planning. The frames hold the potential for what the spaces will become—rooms filled with laughter, walls adorned with art, and windows framing the city's skyline.

Through cutting and framing, the container sheds its identity as a vessel of commerce and gains a new persona as a vessel for life. The architect, in this transformative process, is both surgeon and poet, shaping the steel with an understanding of its nature and a vision of its destiny. The container home, once a mere box, becomes a statement—a declaration of innovative living, a rebuke to the wastefulness of traditional construction, and an ode to the beauty of transformation.

As these modified containers come together, they form more than a structure; they form a narrative of change. They stand as proof of what can be achieved when an architect, armed with tools and vision, approaches a simple container with the intent to create not just a home but a piece of the future. This is the art of cutting and framing in the world of container homes. In this process, every choice, every cut, and every frame are a deliberate step towards crafting a sustainable, minimalist, and innovative living space in the heart of the urban environment.

Insulation and Weatherproofing

Embarking on the journey of transforming a shipping container into a cozy, livable space is akin to tailoring an exquisite garment. It's not merely about the external appearance; the true essence lies in the lining, the internal structure that provides comfort and protection. This is what insulation and weatherproofing do for container homes, creating a haven that is impervious to the whims of weather while upholding the ethos of sustainability and efficiency that our modern architect cherishes.

Insulation is the silent guardian of any home, and in a container, its role is amplified. Steel, the skeletal structure of our container, is a conductor of temperature. Left unattended, it will transmit the searing heat of summer and the biting cold of winter right into the marrow of the dwelling. Insulation, therefore, must be approached with a blend of scientific understanding and artistic finesse.

The choices available marry environmental stewardship with advanced technology. Spray foam insulation adheres to the interior corrugated walls seamlessly, creating an impenetrable barrier that molds itself to every ridge and valley of the container's interior. Its high R-value—a measure of thermal resistance—assures a consistent internal climate, providing an oasis of comfort. For the advocate of natural materials, sheep's wool or denim offers a sustainable and biodegradable alternative, their fibers interlocking to trap air and warmth, a whisper of nature's genius within the industrial heart of the container.

Weatherproofing is the container's shield against nature's elements. It starts with a robust roof coating, a reflective layer that repels the sun's relentless rays, coupled with a seamless moisture barrier that wards off rain's insidious creep. The container's joints and seams are treated with sealants that are both robust and flexible, accommodating the subtle shifts and movements over time without betraying its fortress-like duties.

Windows and doors, the portals to the outside world, are no longer mere openings but are transformed through double or triple glazing, with frames insulated and sealed, standing vigilant against thermal transfer. These glass guardians permit the caress of sunlight while denying entry to the harsher elements, an interplay of light and warmth that is both efficient and poetic.

The choice of insulation and weatherproofing materials speaks volumes of the inhabitant's values. Recycled materials, like cork panels, offer a duality of purpose, providing exceptional thermal regulation and a texture that is visually and tactilely pleasing. Sustainable rigid foam boards, made from renewable resources, not only insulate but also bear witness to the occupant's commitment to a greener future.

Each container home, set against the canvas of an urban skyline or tucked in the bosom of a bustling metropolis, is a testament to the vision of its creator. The careful application of insulation and weatherproofing transforms the once harsh container into a cocoon, a personal retreat that stands resilient against the outside world's fluctuations. It is a tailored space where efficiency meets comfort, where the stark industrial gives way to the warmth of a personal habitat.

In crafting these homes, the architect is the composer and the container his orchestra, each element from insulation to sealant a note in the symphony of sustainable living. It's a performance of materials and technologies, each chosen not just for their function but for their contribution to the more fantastic melody of environmental consciousness.

These homes are not mere structures; they are living, breathing entities, protected from the elements by a skin that is as much a barrier as it is a statement. Insulation and weatherproofing are not hidden aspects of construction but integral parts of the home's identity, as crucial to its form as to its function.

n the end, the insulation and weatherproofing of a container home are the silent verses in the poetry of sustainable architecture. They are the unsung heroes that transform a container from a cold, echoing shell into a warm embrace. Through thoughtful application and careful selection of materials, the architect turns a humble shipping container into a bulwark of comfort. This home not only stands against the storms of nature but also stands as a beacon of innovative, sustainable living in the heart of the city.

Chapter 8

Constructing the Home

The Assembly Process

Constructing a home from shipping containers is a symphony of engineering and artistry, a process that transforms the mundane into the magnificent. It's where precision and imagination intersect to redefine the essence of a dwelling. For an architect, it's a performance, each step choreographed to bring to life a vision that marries sustainability with cutting-edge design. The assembly of a shipping container home isn't just about putting pieces together—it's an act of alchemy that turns steel boxes into spaces of living, breathing art.

In the cool, crisp dawn, the site awakens. The prepared foundation awaits the arrival of its incumbent structures. The containers, having lived past lives on the open seas, now find their resting ground. They are meticulously maneuvered into place, each positioning critical to the architect's blueprint. This is a moment of true convergence, where the potential of modular living becomes tangible, a translation from paper to reality, from concept to concrete form.

Anchoring the containers to the foundation is the first decree in this assembly. This anchorage is not merely physical—it's symbolic of the home's future stability and resilience. Steel marries concrete in an enduring bond as each bolt, each weld, joins the materials in a permanent embrace. As the architect oversees this union, a vision long-held in the mind's eye starts taking shape in steel and space.

The containers, with their pre-modified facades for doors and windows, align with an elegance that belies their industrial origin. The foresight in design and the precision of earlier modifications now come to the forefront. What once was a series of isolated adjustments now reveals itself as a holistic and harmonious design. The structural frame, like the skeleton of some industrial leviathan, begins to flesh out into a home.

Welding the containers is a gesture that fuses the strength of metal with the strength of design. It is a declaration of permanence; each sparks a testament to the home's enduring nature. The architect watches as the containers are transformed, no longer discrete units but parts of a larger, living whole. Insulation is nestled into the walls, a blanket that promises comfort and efficiency, a whisper of the life that will soon flow within these metallic veins.

Cladding the exterior becomes a statement of intent. The corrugated metal surfaces, which once carried the marks of global journeys, are now canvases awaiting their transformation. The architect's choice of materials speaks volumes—sustainability and aesthetics are no longer mere concepts but are woven into the fabric of the building itself. Cladding protects and decorates, conferring identity and character upon the once-uniform container walls.

Within the interior, the hollow resonance of vacant containers is replaced with the quiet bustle of construction. Staircases are introduced to connect the stratified levels, partitions rise to define rooms, and fixtures are strategically placed to create ambiance. The network of electrical and plumbing runs is routed with precision, integrating the containers' industrial heritage into the home's modern functionality.

As the assembly process draws to its close, what emerges is not a mere aggregation of shipping containers but a home. The final bolt tightened, the last sweep of the inspector's gaze through the halls, and the structure was complete. It stands as a beacon of innovative design, a testament to the ingenuity of modern architecture, and a mirror reflecting the architect's passion for sustainable living.

The architect, at the culmination of this process, understands that this is more than just the conclusion of construction. It is the beginning of a new chapter, as the container home is poised to become a dynamic participant in a family's history, a showcase of innovation, and a profound statement in the narrative of modern living.

This assembly process is more than a technical endeavor; it is the architect's hand extended into the future, crafting a legacy in metal, space, and light. The shipping container home stands ready, a testament to what architecture can aspire to when it embraces the principles of sustainability, the promise of affordability, and the poetry of minimalist design.

Adding Extensions and Multiple Levels

In the architectural realm, the allure of shipping container homes lies not just in their eco-friendliness or their chic industrial aesthetic but profoundly in their innate modularity. It's this transformative adaptability that empowers architects to sculpt with space, creating homes that are as expansively unique as the individuals who inhabit them. "Adding Extensions and Multiple Levels" to a container home is akin to composing a symphony—each container a note, each level a harmony, coming together in a crescendo of innovation and design.

When envisioning a multi-tiered home, one is crafting a vertical narrative, a structure that rises to meet the sky with the same ease as it sprawls across the earth. The process begins with the strategic stacking of containers. Like building blocks in the hands of a master, they are carefully positioned, ensuring that the joints and seams align with surgical precision. This alignment is critical, for the integrity of the home hinges upon the strength of its bonds.

As extensions branch out from the core, they carry with them the ethos of the home's design—a seamless flow of interior and exterior spaces, a dance of light and shadow. These extensions serve not just as additional living spaces but as a physical manifestation of the home's connectivity to its surroundings. Be it a cantilevered bedroom reaching toward a scenic view, a glass-encased sunroom soaking in the daylight, or a patio that serves as a natural continuation of the living area, each extension is a declaration of the home's character.

When it comes to adding levels, the vertical expanse of the home is a canvas for the architect's vision. The structure does not merely grow taller; it evolves, it matures. Each level is an opportunity to explore a different facet of design and another aspect of functionality. The lower levels may anchor the home in its pragmatism—garages, storage, perhaps guest accommodations—while the upper tiers aspire to the panoramic, hosting living spaces that offer reprieve and vistas that nourish the soul.

The marriage of containers, when creating multiple levels, requires a dance between strength and delicacy. Reinforcement becomes paramount, as the containers are inherently strong but not invincible. Steel beams crisscross at calculated intervals, bearing the load and dispersing the forces that act upon this vertical village. The architectural heart beats with the rhythm of practicality, ensuring safety and stability are never compromised.

Navigating the staircase of a multi-leveled container home is an experience of transition, moving from one environment to another, each with its distinct ambiance. These transitions are thoughtfully curated—perhaps a burst of natural light as one ascends or a subtle shift in materials that speaks to a change in purpose. The journey from one floor to the next is not merely a physical movement; it is an emotional journey, a narrative woven into the fabric of the home.

In multi-leveled container homes, the rooftop often becomes a realm of possibility. It may evolve into a garden, a terrace, or a retreat that offers communion with the elements. Here, one might reflect under the open sky or entertain as the cityscape unfurls around them. It's not just a space; it's an escape, a testament to the upward extension not just of the home but of the spirit of those who dwell within.

Adding extensions and multiple levels to a container home is not simply an act of construction; it is an act of creation. Each container, each level, and each extension are a brush stroke in a more significant masterpiece. The architect, in his symphony of metal and space, plays with gravity and grace, creating a home that defies convention and embraces the zenith of modern, sustainable living.

In the end, as the architect steps back to survey this bold, dimensional feat, there is a quiet acknowledgment of the power of modularity—a concept that allowed him to transform the simple into the sublime, the humble container into a bastion of vertical living. The home, with its extensions and levels, stands not just as a structure but as a bold declaration of the architect's vision, a beacon of innovative design, and a vessel of the life that will resonate within its walls for years to come.

Chapter 9

Plumbing and Electrical Work

Water Systems and Conservation

In the heart of an architect who harmonizes with the rhythms of sustainability lies the profound understanding that water is not just a utility but a precious resource that demands respect and innovative stewardship. The chapter on "Water Systems and Conservation" in the context of shipping container homes is more than a guide; it's a manifesto that embodies the spirit of modern architectural responsibility. It beckons us to weave conservation into our designs as seamlessly as we integrate the walls that define our spaces.

As you embark on plumbing and integrating water systems into your shipping container home, envision each drop of water as a renewable resource, circulating through the veins of your home with purpose and efficiency. The aim is to create a system where water is not used once but is a participant in a continuous cycle of use, reuse, and replenishment. This cycle begins with the source—whether it be from the municipal supply, collected rainwater, or even greywater systems, the source dictates the system's design.

The sustainable architect views the home as a living organism, with water as its lifeblood. Therefore, the flow within must be well-spent but conservational. Low-flow fixtures become not an afterthought but a fundamental component of your design. These fixtures, along with other water-saving appliances, are selected with the meticulousness of a painter choosing their palette—a careful selection that balances aesthetics with the ethics of conservation.

The narrative of water within your container home then expands to include rainwater harvesting systems. The home, like a tree, reaches out with its canopy—be it the roof or specialized catchment systems—to gather the rainfall. This water, once captured, is channeled, filtered, and repurposed, serving needs from irrigation to sanitation. The architect's design becomes not only a shelter but a reservoir, a proactive participant in water conservation.

Greywater systems echo the ethos of maximizing utility. Water from sinks, showers, and washing machines is given a second life. Through filtration and safe redistribution, this greywater nourishes gardens and landscapes that envelop the home, fostering a green sanctuary that is both a visual splendor and a testament to sustainable practices.

Hot water demands in a sustainable home are addressed with the integration of on-demand water heaters and solar heating systems. These are not merely installations but are carefully curated choices that reflect the home's alignment with the principle of energy conservation. The water is heated efficiently, reducing waste, and is delivered promptly to where it is needed, eliminating the needless loss that comes with outdated systems.

In the spirit of conservation, the very pipelines that form the circulatory system of your home are insulated with precision. This ensures that thermal efficiency is upheld and every degree of heat is cherished and utilized, not lost to the ambiance.

Monitoring and managing water usage is the final, crucial thread in the tapestry of your water systems. Smart home technologies offer a symphony of sensors and meters that provide real-time data, granting the ability to fine-tune consumption patterns, detect leaks, and maintain informed stewardship over this vital resource.

Through these layers of design and innovation, the water system in a shipping container home becomes a paradigm of conservation. It stands as a beacon, guiding the way towards a future where homes not only shelter but sustain, where architects not only design but protect, and where every inhabitant lives not above the environment but in concert with it.

The construction of a container home, therefore, is more than the assembly of steel and insulation; it is the creation of a micro-ecosystem, a small but significant bastion of sustainability. At the core of this ecosystem is a water system designed with the foresight, care, and ingenuity that honors the fluid mosaic of modern life and the timeless flow of nature itself. As you, the architect, draft the blueprints of these homes, you are not just etching out spaces; you are drawing from the well of innovation, crafting systems that will sustain lives while safeguarding the drop of water that is as vital as the air we breathe.

Electrical Systems for Off-grid Living

Imagine harnessing the sun's golden energy, the whispering wind, or even the silent power resting in the Earth's thermal embrace to electrify your home. For the visionary architect, creating an off-grid electrical system is not just about cutting ties with the public utilities; it's about forging a self-sufficient sanctuary that stands as a testament to human ingenuity and respect for the Earth.

When you embark on designing an off-grid electrical system for a shipping container home, you embark on a journey that is both challenging and rewarding. This is not merely a technical endeavor; it's a canvas where your design skills merge with the latest in sustainable technology to create a living space that is autonomous, efficient, and harmoniously integrated with its environment.

Solar Power: The Heartbeat of Off-grid Living

Solar power is often the cornerstone of off-grid electrical systems. The container home, with its robust and flat rooftop, presents a perfect platform for photovoltaic panels. These silent sentinels collect the sun's bounty, converting it into electrical energy that powers daily life. But it's not just about placing panels atop your container home; it's about understanding the dance of the sun across the sky, the tilt and orientation of panels for optimal energy harvest, and the symphony of charge controllers, batteries, and inverters that store and manage this precious energy.

The solar setup becomes an integrated part of the home's design, a feature that is as aesthetically pleasing as it is functional. The power storage—where the heart of your solar system holds the sun's captured energy—is designed to be both accessible for maintenance and seamlessly integrated into the home's layout. Batteries are chosen not just for their capacity but for their longevity, environmental impact, and the way they complement the home's energy needs and usage patterns.

Wind Turbines: The Whispers of Self-sufficiency

In areas where the wind is as much a part of the landscape as the Earth itself, wind turbines stand like modern-day windmills. These turbines, whether perched atop a mast or integrated into the building's architecture, are not simply installations; they are expressions of a design philosophy that embraces the air as a source of power. In your design, you consider not only the turbine's power generation capabilities but also its interplay with the home's aesthetics and its acoustic footprint, ensuring that it adds to rather than detracts from the living experience.

Geothermal Systems: The Earth's Quiet Offering

Where the situation allows, geothermal systems offer a stable and continuous source of energy. This is where your design delves deep into the Earth, tapping into the thermal consistency of the ground to both heat and cool the home. The container home, then, is not just an object upon the land but a structure that reaches into the land, drawing from its constant temperature to reduce the reliance on traditional energy sources.

The Integration of Energy Systems

In the true spirit of off-grid living, no single source of energy is relied upon entirely. Your design philosophy brings together these diverse energy systems—solar, wind, and geothermal—into a cohesive unit. This integrated approach ensures that when the sun sets or the wind stills, the home remains a beacon of warmth and light. The electrical system you design is robust, redundant, and resilient, capable of adapting to the changing moods of nature while providing continuous power.

Smart Energy Management: The Pulse of the Home

Within the walls of your container home, intelligent systems pulse with the current of innovation. These systems are the brain of the home, continuously monitoring energy consumption, optimizing the use of available power, and ensuring that the resident's energy footprint is as light as possible. You design not just for the present but for a future where the home learns and adapts, where software updates enhance efficiency, and where the owner has real-time insight into their energy ecosystem.

The off-grid electrical system you create for your shipping container home is a silent revolution, a declaration of independence from the grid. It's a commitment to a lifestyle that values self-reliance, sustainability, and harmony with the environment. Your designs do not shout; they whisper the future of home energy, a future that is as exciting as it is essential in our journey towards a more sustainable world.

Chapter 10

Heating and Cooling

Passive Solar Design

As we explore the concept of passive solar design within the context of shipping container homes, we embark on a journey of environmental harmony. This journey is not only about the aesthetics of the space we occupy but also about a seamless blend of form and function that respects the ebb and flow of the natural world. The practice of passive solar design transforms the home into a living entity, responsive to the nuances of light and season, a testament to an architect's foresight and ingenuity.

In the sphere of shipping container architecture, passive solar design takes on heightened significance. These steel structures, once mere cogs in the global trade machine, are repurposed into habitable art forms that interact with the sun's trajectory. The brilliance of passive solar design lies in its simplicity—the strategic orientation of the container, the mindful placement of windows, and the selection of materials all coalesce to capture or repel the sun's heat as desired.

The shipping container home, oriented to capitalize on the sun's journey, becomes a haven of energy efficiency. South-facing windows are no random choice; they are the soul of the home, welcoming the winter sun's embrace. These glazed apertures are not merely windows but gateways for the sun's warmth to penetrate the living space, charging the thermal mass within. This mass, be it a robust concrete floor, a densely packed earth wall, or even phase-changing materials, serves as the silent steward of heat. During the day, it is a sponge, soaking up solar energy, and as night falls, it is a gentle heart, radiating warmth back into space.

Yet, passive solar design is not solely about welcoming the sun; it is equally about shading and cooling, a concept perfectly embodied by the summer sun's exclusion. Overhangs, thoughtfully designed for their length and depth, play their part in shielding and cooling, as do strategically placed trees or vegetative screens that contribute shade and transpiration cooling. This is where design marries nature, creating spaces that are inherently equipped to fend off the swelter of summer days.

The intricate dance between the home and the sun is further nuanced by the very geometry of the container home itself. The pitch of the roof, the depth of the eaves, and the placement of skylights are orchestrated with the sun's path in mind. This precision ensures that the low winter sun is a welcome guest while the high summer sun is respectfully kept at bay. Through this intelligent design, the need for mechanical heating and cooling is minimized, allowing nature to provide comfort.

Materials, the very sinews of passive solar design, are chosen not just for their physical properties but also for their environmental narratives. They stand as silent witnesses to the home's green philosophy, their thermal attributes working in concert with the climate. High thermal mass materials embody sustainability; they absorb the day's heat, mitigating temperature swings and reducing the carbon footprint of the home.

Ventilation is the unseen maestro of this symphony, choreographing air flow through the home to purge unwanted heat and draw in cooler night air. Operable windows, skylights, and strategically placed vents are not mere openings but are integral components of a natural cooling system.

Designing for the future means envisioning a home that not only withstands the test of time but also responds to the changing climates and seasons. This anticipatory approach is embedded in the ethos of passive solar design, where the home is a dynamic entity, adapting and evolving with its environment. The passive solar container home, thus, stands as a beacon of sustainability—a physical manifestation of the philosophy of living with, rather than against, the rhythms of nature.

This approach extends beyond technicalities; it speaks to the heart of what it means to create spaces for living. Passive solar design in shipping container homes is not just about smart energy use; it is a lifestyle choice, a commitment to an ethos that values restraint, respect for natural resources, and a deep-seated appreciation for the inherent beauty of our environment. As an architect dedicated to pioneering sustainable and innovative building practices, passive solar design empowers you to craft spaces that are not only efficient and elegant but also deeply resonant with the principles of ecological stewardship. Your creation is not a mere dwelling but a harmonious space, tuned to the ancient rhythm of sun and shadow, warmth and coolness—a home that is both a sanctuary and a statement, an ode to the sun's quiet power.

HVAC Options for Container Homes

Heating, Ventilation, and Air Conditioning (HVAC) systems in shipping container homes are a testament to the versatility of this growing architectural trend. These compact and efficient living spaces, emerging from the blueprint of sustainability, require HVAC solutions that not only embrace the unique challenges of container homes but also mirror the values of their inhabitants.

Within the metal walls of a container, the traditional HVAC system is reimagined. It's not about installing an off-the-shelf unit but about tailoring a system that fits the home like a glove. These systems are designed to work with the container's intrinsic properties — its superb air and watertight nature and excellent structural strength — to provide a living environment that stands up to both the scorching heat of summer and the biting cold of winter.

Selecting the right HVAC system for a container home goes beyond mere temperature control; it's about creating a micro-climate within a home that is as dynamic and adaptable as its owners. The most common systems in the market — split systems, window units, and central air — all have their pros and cons. Still, they must be evaluated not just for efficiency but for their fit within the minimalist and sustainable ethos of container living.

For the architect who embraces both innovation and practicality, ductless mini-split systems are often the favored choice. They offer a sleek and unobtrusive profile that harmonizes with the clean lines of a container home. Their ability to provide both heating and cooling within a single unit also aligns with the minimalist philosophy, reducing clutter and maximizing space. Mini-splits are celebrated for their zone-specific climate control, offering the flexibility to heat or cool individual rooms based on occupancy, a boon for the environmentally conscious.

But innovation continues beyond there. For those looking to push the envelope, radiant floor heating systems are making waves in the container home community. This system transforms the floor into a radiant heating source, gently and evenly increasing the temperature of a room from the ground up. The result is a comfort that is not only felt but also seen in the absence of unsightly vents and ductwork. The container's metal composition becomes an ally, conducting the warmth throughout the space with surprising efficiency.

In climates where the air carries a chill, wood-burning stoves have seen a resurgence, especially in container homes where space is at a premium. Their small footprint and ability to provide a cozy heat source are perfect for the architect seeking a touch of rustic charm without sacrificing functionality. Moreover, when used responsibly with sustainably sourced wood, they can be an environmentally considerate heating option.

On the ventilation front, it's crucial to ensure that the air inside a container home remains fresh and free of condensation — a challenge given the tight seal of the container. Heat Recovery Ventilators (HRV) or Energy Recovery Ventilators (ERV) come into play here, conserving energy while maintaining air quality. They work by extracting stale air and, in the process, reclaiming its heat to warm the incoming fresh air. This technology speaks to the heart of sustainable living, echoing a commitment to energy conservation.

The conversation about HVAC in container homes would be complete with a touch on innovations in smart home technology. Programmable thermostats, when synchronized with an HVAC system, allow precise control over the home's environment, learning the homeowner's preferences and adjusting accordingly for optimum comfort and efficiency. This intelligent adaptation is not just a convenience but a reflection of a life where technology and sustainability are intertwined.

Ultimately, the choice of HVAC in a container home is deeply personal and reflects the architect's values and the homeowner's lifestyle. It's a decision that balances comfort with consciousness and practicality with passion for the planet. As these structures evolve from their industrial origins into bespoke habitats, so too do the systems that imbue them with life. The container home, a symbol of innovation and resilience, demands an HVAC system that is equally robust and responsive — an integral part of a home that is not only a dwelling but a declaration of sustainable, intentional living.

Chapter 11

Interior Design and Maximizing Space

Multifunctional Furniture

In the realm of container homes, where every inch is precious, the magic of multifunctional furniture becomes not just a feature of design but a profound statement of lifestyle. This transformative furniture acts as the pivotal point where form meets function, where the sleek contours of modern aesthetics blend with the sharp efficiency of utility.

For the architect threading the needle between innovation and practicality, multifunctional furniture is the thread that sews together space-saving solutions with the tapestry of sustainable living. These pieces are not merely furniture; they are functional sculptures capable of morphing to the needs of the moment without sacrificing an ounce of style or comfort.

Take, for example, the bed that seamlessly converts into a desk. By day, it's the cornerstone of a home office, the platform of productivity; by night, it retracts into a haven of rest. Or consider the dining table that can pivot, fold, and transform into a sleek workstation or a coffee table, bridging the divide between mealtimes and leisure.

The true beauty of these pieces lies not just in their functionality but in their potential to expand the living area. A sofa that unfolds into a guest bed, complete with hidden storage for linens, not only provides a comfortable sleep solution but also leverages unused space. This is especially crucial in a container home, where the footprint is finite, and every element must be as resourceful as its owner.

When designing a container home, an architect must approach the interior with a curator's eye, selecting pieces that resonate with the client's ethos. The furniture must reflect the minimalist core of container living, where less is indeed more, where the air in the room is as much a part of the décor as the objects that fill it.

Beyond the practicalities, multifunctional furniture is a nod to the future, an acknowledgment that space, particularly in urban environments, is at a premium. It's a trend that answers the call of rising populations and shrinking living quarters, a smart response to the challenges of modern housing.

This furniture also speaks to the heart of personal expression. In a container home, the limitations of space force a focus on what's truly essential. Each piece of furniture must earn its place not just through utility but through aesthetics and personal connection. It's about creating a dialogue between the inhabitant and their environment, where every fold, every slide, and every transformation is an act of engagement. This deliberate choice shapes the living space.

In selecting these pieces, the container homeowner is presented with a plethora of choices, from the sleek and modern to the rustic and reclaimed. Materials range from renewable bamboo to recycled plastics and metals, each with its own story, each contributing to the narrative of the home. The furniture becomes a conversation starter, a point of interest that reflects the homeowner's commitment to sustainability and smart design.

However, it's not just about the individual pieces; it's about how they interact with the container home's environment. The color palette, the textures, the lines — they all work in concert to create a harmonious space. The furniture, in its multiple forms, must dance to the same rhythm as the architecture itself, complementing the container's industrial origins while softening the space to make it livable and warm.

For the modern architect and homeowner, these pieces are an opportunity to push the boundaries of what's possible within the confines of a compact living space. It's a challenge that calls for creativity and innovation, a chance to redefine the very concept of home furniture.

Multifunctional furniture in container homes is not just about saving space; it's about elevating the quality of life within that space. It's about making every square foot count, about transforming the ordinary into the extraordinary. As these homes continue to carve out their niche in the housing market, the furniture within them stands as a testament to the ingenuity and spirit of those who choose to live within the corrugated walls of what was once a simple shipping container.

Storage Solutions

The artistry of storage in the context of container homes is akin to the meticulous choreography of a ballet. Every leap and bound across the stage are calculated, much like every storage solution in a container home must be deliberate, serving a function while maintaining the elegance of space. The architect delving into the design of these innovative homes must see beyond the mere containment of items; they must envision storage as an integral component of the living space, as vital as the walls that form the rooms themselves.

In the fabric of a container home's interior design, storage solutions are not afterthoughts; they are interwoven into the very essence of the home, creating a seamless blend of form and function. The tailored solutions champion the principles of minimalism and sustainability—mantras for the modern architect and the conscious dweller.

Consider the kitchen, the heart of the home, where storage must cater to both utility and aesthetics. Here, pull-out cabinets and hidden compartments emerge from the sleek lines, ensuring that every utensil and appliance has a home within a home. The integration of spice racks inside cupboard doors, retractable shelving, and toe-kick drawers utilizes every possible nook, transforming dead space into dynamic zones of storage.

The bedroom, a sanctuary of solitude and silence, benefits from built-in platforms where the space beneath the mattress, typically neglected, becomes a discrete storeroom for seasonal clothing or infrequently used items. Closets with customizable organization systems adapt to the personal wardrobe of the inhabitant, with adjustable shelving and rods, ensuring that from the most cumbersome winter coat to the delicate hang of a silk scarf, there is a designated space.

Living areas, too, serve a dual purpose, with entertainment units designed to house not only the technology that connects us to the world but also the collections that tell our story. Bookshelves wrap around door frames, stretching towards the ceiling—spaces traditionally unused now hold literature, artifacts, and memories. Even seating can double as storage, with benches opening up to reveal compartments for the assortment of daily life.

The bathroom, often the most challenging space to keep uncluttered, becomes a model of efficiency with mirrored medicine cabinets that extend into the wall cavity, recessed shelving in showers, and vanity drawers with compartments specifically molded for toiletries. These solutions, refined and discreet, contribute to the tranquility of the space.

Incorporating storage into the structural elements of the home also presents an opportunity to redefine boundaries. Staircases become more than a means to traverse levels—they evolve into libraries, display spaces, or drawers for items that benefit from being tucked away yet remaining accessible.

The use of vertical space is another fundamental concept in container home storage. The precious square footage at ground level is conserved by employing the walls themselves as storage—hanging bicycles, vertical gardens that double as pantry space, and drop-down tables that fold away when not in use are just a few examples of this principle in practice.

For the architect, these storage solutions are a canvas for creativity. The materials chosen speak to the sustainable ethos of the container home. Reclaimed wood, metal from decommissioned ships, and even repurposed fixtures from other architectural projects lend a story to the storage, each piece resonating with a history that enriches the home's narrative.

The finishing of these storage areas is as important as their function. A cohesive color scheme, a play on textures, and lighting designed to highlight and enhance, not just illuminate, are crucial considerations. The architect's vision for these spaces is one where the harmony between living area and storage is indistinguishable—one flows into the other, creating a living experience that is both practical and poetic.

Ultimately, the container home stands as a paradigm of intentional living, where every aspect of its design, including storage, is a testament to a lifestyle that values the essence of simplicity and the elegance of efficiency. It's a compact symphony where each storage solution is a note that contributes to the greater harmony of the home. For the modern professional, the appeal of this efficient, innovative approach to living space is as much a reflection of their values as it is of their aesthetic—the container home, with its ingenious storage solutions, becomes a personal manifesto, a three-dimensional representation of their worldview.

Chapter 12

Exterior Finishes and Considerations

Cladding Options

In the architectural odyssey of creating a shipping container home, the alchemy lies in the harmonious fusion of aesthetics and endurance. Cladding, the skin of the home, is not merely a cosmetic afterthought; it is the vital narrative that announces the home's character to the world while shielding its structural integrity. As we delve into the cladding options for your container home, we aren't just picking out a coat for the coming winter; we are selecting the textures, colors, and materials that will define the domicile's identity.

As an architect at the zenith of modern innovation, one recognizes that the facade of a shipping container home is a canvas awaiting its masterpiece. The materials you select speak volumes about the values held within—sustainability, resilience, and a daring to defy conventional aesthetics.

In a world where the container home stands as a testament to repurposing and resilience, wood cladding emerges as a favorite. It's a nod to nature, a way to soften the industrial edges and insulate the soul of the home in warmth. From reclaimed timber to sustainable bamboo, wood can be both a classic homage to traditional design and a modern, eco-friendly statement.

Metal, the kin of the container itself, offers a sleek, reflective surface that mirrors the innovation of container living. Corrugated steel can maintain the industrial heritage, while copper or zinc can evolve with the elements, developing a patina that tells a story of time and exposure. It's for the architect who sees beauty in transformation and values the longevity of materials.

Then, there's the robust character of stone cladding—a material that whispers tales of ancient fortresses and timeless strength. It stands unyielding against the elements and provides an insulating embrace against the cold. Whether it's the rustic appeal of fieldstone or the sleek precision of cut granite, stone cladding elevates the container home to a monument of enduring stability.

For those whose palette favors a more innovative approach, composite materials offer a playground of variety. These can be engineered to provide superior insulation, fire resistance, and a spectrum of finishes from matte to lustrous. They champion the contemporary and celebrate the forward-thinking spirit of container home living.

One must not overlook the chameleon qualities of cementitious fiberboards, able to mimic wood or concrete with ease, and the versatility of glass as a cladding material—transparent or frosted, it invites light to play a central role in the design, creating a home that converses with the sun and dances with shadows.

For the architect whose designs whisper of the future, the embrace of smart cladding materials—those that clean the air, harvest solar energy or change hue with the touch of an app—is the ultimate testament to the potential of container homes. It's where sustainability leaps into the realm of the magical, turning homes into active participants in energy conservation and environmental stewardship.

Each cladding choice weaves its narrative, one that is intrinsically linked to the personality of the home and its occupants. Whether it be the rustic allure of weathered cedar or the high-tech sheen of photovoltaic panels, the cladding of a container home is more than a shell; it is a declaration of intent, a carefully crafted poem composed in the language of materials.

And yet, with every choice comes the need for careful consideration. The cladding must not only captivate but also protect. It must stand vigilant against the vagaries of weather, the caress of the sun, and the embrace of the frost. In choosing the cladding for a container home, we weigh the thermal properties, the ease of installation, the maintenance demands, and, crucially, the environmental impact of production and eventual disposal.

As an architect, you are the steward of these considerations, tasked with merging the client's vision with the unforgiving realities of physics and the finite bounty of our planet. Your choices in cladding are the synthesis of this complex equation, balancing desire with duty and dreams with durability.

Let the cladding you choose for your container homes be a testament to your craft—a harmonious blend of purpose and passion that stands proud against the skyline, inviting the gaze of passersby and the whisper of the winds with equal aplomb.

Decking and Outdoor Living Spaces

In the grand narrative of container home design, decking, and outdoor living spaces are the bridges between the raw integrity of industrial form and the organic flow of natural habitat. These spaces are a breath of fresh air in the denser urban fabric where our green sanctuaries are the currency of wellbeing. They represent an architectural interlude, where the indoor rigor of steel yields the outdoor serenity of wood, stone, and greenery.

For the discerning architect, the design of these transitional areas is not an afterthought but a deliberate extension of the living space. The decking around a container home is where structure meets spontaneity, where straight lines bend to the organic contours of nature, and where the container's inherent modularity finds its match in the malleable grace of outdoor design.

Decking material is chosen with a nod to environmental responsibility and an eye on aesthetic versatility. Reclaimed wood offers a story with every grain, a history that adds depth to the modernity of the container. Composite materials stand as a testament to innovation, providing durable, low-maintenance platforms upon which life unfolds. They exist in harmony with the container home, reflecting its values of sustainability and its essence of reinvention.

The design must account for the multi-functionality of the space. It is here that morning yoga greets the dawn, where al fresco dining encounters dusk, and where the stillness of evening contemplation meets the night sky. For the outdoor space to be genuinely integral to the container home, it must be as flexible as the life it hosts. Built-in seating that doubles as storage, adjustable shading to dance with the sun's whims, and modular garden units to cultivate herbs or blooms—all become part of a larger symphony of functional beauty.

The outdoor living space is also a haven for sustainable practices. The inclusion of a rainwater collection system within the deck's architecture, for instance, not only emphasizes the eco-consciousness of the design but serves a practical purpose in watering gardens or servicing outdoor utilities. Lighting, too, is an area where the container home's outdoor space can shine—solar-powered LED fixtures can illuminate the night with minimal impact on the environment.

As we venture beyond the bounds of the deck, the living space expands into the realm of gardens and gathering spots. Fire pits crafted from repurposed materials ignite conversations and camaraderie, while vertical gardens on the container walls bring life to every square inch available. This outdoor realm is an ecosystem in itself, designed to thrive in the urban landscape, offering a reprieve from concrete and a chorus of nature in the heart of the city.

The astute architect knows that these spaces must be adaptive and able to evolve with the shifting patterns of life. Thus, the deck and its adjuncts are designed for modularity, able to be reconfigured as the needs of the home and its inhabitants morph through time. They are spaces of connection—not just between people and the environment, but between present needs and future possibilities.

In the greater context of the container home, the outdoor space is where the rigid becomes reflective, where the container's industrial past transmutes into a pastoral present. It's an alchemy of open skies and the container's steel, of wind's whisper through leaves and the echo of urban life. This is the realm where our architect creates not just a home but a habitat—a sanctuary where the boundaries of interior and exterior blur into a seamless expanse of living art.

For those who inhabit these spaces, they are the locales of life's quieter moments and grand celebrations. These are the settings of solitude and socializing, where the art of living is practiced in its most genuine form. The outdoor living space of a container home is a portrait of its occupants—complex, ever-changing, and vibrantly alive.

Here, in the dialogue between inside and out, we find the true essence of the container home—not as an isolated unit but as a fluid component of a larger ecosystem. It is a testament to the belief that architecture is not just about structures but about crafting environments that resonate with the rhythm of life they house. The decking and outdoor spaces, therefore, are not mere appendages but integral chapters in the story of container home living, each board laid, each plant nurtured, a verse in the poetry of sustainable habitation.

Chapter 13

Landscaping and Permaculture

Designing an Eco-Friendly Landscape

As architects, we are curators of space, and when it comes to the land that cradles our creations, we bear a responsibility to honor and uplift its natural essence. Designing an eco-friendly landscape for a shipping container home is not merely a matter of aesthetics but a profound exercise in environmental stewardship and permaculture principles.

The eco-friendly landscape is an extension of the home where humans and habitats coalesce with a shared spirit of conservation and beauty. This landscape is not dominated by rigid lines or manicured lawns, which often stand as silent testimonials to human control over nature. Instead, it's a canvas where biodiversity, water efficiency, and indigenous flora are the celebrated artists.

In the architectural journey of a shipping container home, the landscape is where the metallic meets the organic. The eco-friendly landscape is designed to create a symbiotic relationship with the container's geometry, blending the rugged edges into the soft contours of the land. It is a space that captures rainwater to nurture the ground, uses native plants to fortify the soil, and encourages wildlife to become an integral part of the living environment.

Permaculture is the heartbeat of this landscape design—a philosophy that intertwines with the very essence of shipping container homes. It is a design science rooted in the observation of natural ecosystems, a discipline that mimics the resilience and self-sustaining properties of the wild. Every plant, path, and pond are placed with purpose, ensuring that the land not only thrives but regenerates, creating a self-sustaining loop of abundance.

Selecting vegetation is a process steeped in respect for the local climate and ecology. The plants chosen are not simply decorative; they are native species that belong to the land and require minimal irrigation. These plants are the natural allies of the soil and co-conspirators in the quest to reduce water usage and protect against erosion. They provide food and refuge for local fauna, creating an environment that is not just tolerated by the local wildlife but wholly embraced.

The utilization of organic mulches, the creation of composting systems, and the introduction of beneficial insects all contribute to a robust ecosystem that supports itself. The result is a garden that grows richer with each passing season, a place where the soil is alive with microorganisms and the air vibrates with the wings of pollinators.

The landscape's design also extends to the very materials we use to sculpt it. Recycled materials find new purpose in walkways and retaining walls. The gravel underfoot once belonged to a distant roadway; the stone that edges the garden beds was once part of a demolished building. In this way, the history of humanity is interwoven with the present moment, creating a narrative of renewal and continuity.

Water is cherished like the precious resource it is, with rain gardens and bioswales ingeniously designed to harness and filter runoff and drip irrigation systems stealthily placed to deliver water directly to plant roots. These systems speak to an understanding that every drop of water is a gift and must be managed with care and foresight.

The design of an eco-friendly landscape is a declaration of values, a tangible reflection of the belief that our homes should not impose upon the earth but rather coexist with it. It's a design philosophy that acknowledges that each choice we make—from the selection of a single seed to the configuration of a garden—has an impact far beyond our own backyards.

Creating an eco-friendly landscape around a shipping container home is a bold act of ecological imagination. It is a space that does not just sit on the land but converses with it, listens to it, and learns from it. It is here, in the dance of shadow and light over wildflowers and reclaimed wood, that we find a vision of the future—a future where our homes are not only shelters but also stewards of the earth.

As our architect surveys the land, there is a profound understanding that this space is not being "developed" but rather "revealed." The land speaks, and the design responds, creating a landscape that is not just seen but experienced—a living, breathing, thriving testament to the beauty and possibility of an eco-conscious life.

Edible Gardens and Water Features

As an architect with a nuanced appreciation for sustainable living, you understand that a home is not merely a shelter but a multisensory experience that interacts with its inhabitants and their environment. Within the verdant embrace of permaculture, edible gardens, and water features are not just components of a landscape but vital organs of a living, breathing ecosystem centered around a shipping container home.

Edible Gardens: A Feast for the Senses

The concept of an edible garden transcends the traditional vegetable plot. It's an intricate mosaic of fruit-bearing trees, aromatic herbs, and verdant vegetables, all interwoven to create a tapestry that feeds both the body and the aesthetic soul. As one weave through the garden, the rustle of leaves and the hum of diligent pollinators become the soundtrack to a space that is alive with purpose.

In the design of an edible garden, you craft a narrative that begins with the soil—rich, nourishing, and cultivated to support a cornucopia of native edibles. You select plants not just for their yield but for their compatibility with the local climate and their contribution to the ecosystem. A guild of apple trees, underplanted with chives and comfrey, tells a story of symbiotic relationships, where each species supports the other in a delicate dance of give and take.

The garden is laid out with an intimate knowledge of the sun's path, ensuring that each plant receives the light it needs to thrive. Paths meander between raised beds constructed from repurposed materials, their geometry a subtle echo of the container home's linear form. These beds become the stage for a succession of crops that rotate with the seasons, providing a year-round harvest that transforms the kitchen into a repository of fresh, organic produce.

Within this green sanctuary, the architecture of the container home becomes a silent observer, its sleek metal reflecting the myriad greens of the garden. The boundary between dwelling and earth blurs, with trellises leaning against walls and sweet peas curling around the corners, as if the building itself is reaching out to embrace the bounty.

Water Features: The Essence of Serenity

Water, the lifeblood of any landscape, is celebrated in the container home's garden not just as a necessity for growth but as a centerpiece for contemplation and conservation. The water feature—a pond, a fountain, or a stream—becomes a mirror reflecting the changing skies and a habitat for local wildlife. It is both art and instrument, a marriage of form and function that enchants the senses while replenishing the aquifer.

The design of water features is grounded in an ecological ethos, with systems to capture rainwater from the container roof, channeling it through decorative downspouts into a living, breathing aquatic garden. This water is not idle; it is filtered by the roots of water plants, oxygenated by the splash of a waterfall, and ultimately used to irrigate the edible gardens. In this cycle, every drop tells a story of conservation and reverence for nature's gifts.

The sound of water becomes a balm for the urban soul, a reminder of nature's rhythms in the heart of the metropolitan bustle. Whether it's the gentle trickle of a bamboo fountain or the soft whisper of a reed-fringed brook, these water features are the auditory essence of tranquility that defines the spirit of the space.

Integrating Edible Gardens and Water Features

The true artistry of combining edible gardens with water features lies in creating a space where function and form achieve a delicate balance. The reflection of fruit trees on the pond's surface, the sound of water amidst the rustling of the vegetable patch—these sensory experiences are carefully orchestrated to create an environment that is not only sustainable but spiritually satisfying.

Designing these elements requires a conscious intention to forge connections— not just between the container home and its landscape but between individuals and the environment. It's a holistic approach that considers the lifecycle of every element, ensuring that the home's footprint is as nurturing as it is minimal.

As the architect of such a space, you become a storyteller; each design choice is a verse in an epic poem about harmony, sustainability, and life lived in concert with nature. The shipping container home, with its edible gardens and water features, becomes not just a place of residence but a living declaration of a commitment to nourish both the individual and the earth, a home that is truly a sanctuary for growth, reflection, and sustenance.

Chapter 14

Legalities and Building Codes

Navigating Zoning Laws

Navigating the intricacies of zoning laws is a nuanced expedition, one that the architect with a vision for sustainable, minimalist living must undertake with both patience and precision. The architect who ventures into the world of shipping container homes must not only be a master of design but also an adept interpreter of the legal language that shapes our urban landscapes.

The task at hand is not simply a matter of compliance but an intricate dance with the local statutes that govern land use. Zoning laws are not a monolith; they vary from city to city, neighborhood to neighborhood, each with its unique set of expectations and limitations. Understanding these local nuances is paramount, as they are the foundational rules that will either enable or constrain the realization of a shipping container home.

Embarking on this journey requires a meticulous gathering of knowledge. One must delve deep into the local zoning ordinances, engage with city planners, and decipher the complex land use codes that dictate what can be built and where. This investigation often reveals a web of restrictions that might include height limitations, setback requirements, and land usage regulations, all of which are critical to understanding in detail.

The innovative architect must not only grasp the letter of these laws but also engage with their spirit. To win the favor of those who enforce these regulations, it is necessary to present a compelling case that transcends the traditional view of what a home should be. This requires framing the concept of a shipping container home within the context of its benefits: sustainability, affordability, and a unique aesthetic that can enhance the fabric of the existing community.

However, the dialogue with zoning officials is not a monologue; it is a two-way conversation that requires listening as much as it speaks. Building relationships with these gatekeepers is essential, as is the ability to articulate a vision that aligns with the community's values. These conversations can sometimes lead to a reshaping of the project's design, as feedback from officials and community members alike can offer insights that refine and improve the architect's original plan.

When the criticisms of zoning laws present seemingly insurmountable barriers, the quest for variance becomes the path to follow. Securing a variance is a testament to an architect's ability to argue the case for their design as an asset to the community that outweighs the rigidity of existing codes. It is a challenge that tests the architect's ingenuity in finding solutions that satisfy both the creative and legal requirements of the building.

The journey through the maze of zoning laws is often a test of resilience. Each setback encountered and navigated reinforces the architect's commitment to their craft and their vision. When that commitment finally leads to approval, it represents a harmonious agreement between innovation and regulation, a milestone that signifies not just the construction of a home but the creation of a space that is both environmentally responsible and beautifully unique.

As architects, the role is multifaceted; they are designers, negotiators, and sometimes even educators, explaining the virtues of shipping container homes to those who are yet to be acquainted with their potential. They conduct an orchestra of stakeholders, from the community residents to the local officials, ensuring that every voice is heard and that the final design is a symphony that everyone can appreciate.

Navigating zoning laws, therefore, is a journey that encapsulates the essence of being an architect in the modern world. It requires a deft balance between the visionary and the practical, the innovative and the permissible. It is about pushing boundaries while respecting the frameworks that uphold our communities. It is a task that, when done well, doesn't just result in the construction of a home but contributes to the ongoing narrative of sustainable living.

In conclusion, for the architect who aspires to incorporate shipping container homes into their repertoire, mastering the art of navigating zoning laws is not just a necessary skill but a critical aspect of their practice. It involves a deep understanding of local regulations, a capacity to adapt and innovate within legal confines, and the communication skills to bring the community along on the journey. It is through this mastery that the architect can transform a vision of sustainable, minimalist living into a tangible reality, creating spaces that resonate with the ethos of a modern, environmentally conscious society.

Understanding Building Standards and Compliance

When the unconventional beauty of a shipping container home transitions from a sketched vision to the structural bones of a physical abode, it's not merely the architect's ingenuity that's unveiled but also the intricate matrix of building standards and compliance that underpin its existence. For the architect who forges paths within the fertile grounds of innovative housing, the lattice of building codes is not a constraint but a canvas upon which the safety and integrity of sustainable living are drawn.

Building standards are the silent sentinels of the construction world, guardians of quality and safety that demand to be both understood and respected. In the realm of shipping container homes, these standards serve a dual purpose: ensuring the habitability of inventive spaces and fortifying the trust between the architect and those who will call these structures home.

An architect in the urban tableau, grappling with the complexities of modern living and cost-efficient design, knows well the pivotal role of compliance. The International Building Code (IBC), alongside local adaptations, becomes a scripture as sacred as any design blueprint. These codes, while seemingly a labyrinth of clauses and sub-clauses are, in fact, the meticulous annotations of collective wisdom distilled from decades of architectural triumphs and tragedies.

Comprehension of these standards necessitates more than a cursory glance. It demands an immersion into the particulars of structural integrity, where the robustness of a shipping container must meet the rigidity of seismic codes and the suppleness needed to withstand the caprices of climate. The energy codes, an ode to sustainability, must find resonance in the container home's design, whispering through its insulation choices and energy-efficient windows, articulating a home's harmony with the environment.

Fire codes speak to the architect in a language of prevention and protection, instructing on the necessity of egress points and the placement of smoke detectors, a dialogue that ensures the inhabitants' safety is never compromised. Accessibility codes advocate for an inclusive vision, where the embrace of a home is wide enough to welcome all, and living spaces are crafted to serve the needs of diverse occupants.

Navigating these codes, the architect engages in meticulous choreography, where each step of construction is a move toward compliance. From the acoustics inscribed within walls to the air quality that breathes through the home, standards guide the dance. They whisper the parameters of electrical wiring, the nuances of plumbing, and the exactness of load-bearing calculations.

Yet, these standards are not static relics; they are dynamic, evolving with technology and societal shifts. Staying abreast of these changes is not just a professional requirement but a creative stimulus for the architect. The adoption of new materials, the innovative methods of assembly, and the integration of smart technology are all dialogues enriched by an understanding of current codes.

In the pursuit of compliance, the architect's toolbox is expansive. Resources such as the National Fire Protection Association (NFPA) for fire codes, the American Society of Heating, Refrigerating and Air-Conditioning Engineers (ASHRAE) for energy standards, and the American National Standards Institute (ANSI) for accessibility guidelines are not mere references but collaborators in the construction journey.

Examples of compliance are found in the ligaments of the home's design. A container's journey from a vessel of commerce to a vessel for living is marked by these standards. The cutting of a container for a window is more than an architectural flourish; it is a compliance with egress codes. The integration of a ramp is not merely an aesthetic choice but an alignment with accessibility standards—every insulation layer, every bolt, and every joint whispers the narrative of a building code.

To the architect, these standards are not roadblocks but milestones. They do not stifle creativity but rather elevate it, ensuring that the boldness of design never jeopardizes the home's integrity. Compliance becomes not just a legal obligation but a testament to the architect's commitment to quality, sustainability, and the safeguarding of their occupants' well-being.

In sum, understanding building standards and compliance is the hallmark of the architect's prowess. It is through this lens that the container home becomes a paragon of sustainable innovation. This structure stands proudly at the intersection of creativity and responsibility, embodying the very essence of modern architectural ambition.

Chapter 15

Living in a Container Home

Daily Life and Functionality

The allure of container homes is not just in their aesthetic distinctiveness or their nod to sustainable living—it's also found in the pulse of daily life within their metal walls, which are both a sanctuary and a statement. Life in a container home is a composition of function, efficiency, and a connection to the surrounding environment, a symphony played out in steel.

For the visionary architect who resides in the heartbeat of urban innovation, these structures offer an escape from the mundane. The functionality of a container home is its lifeblood, allowing for a streamlined existence that is both pragmatic and poetic. The container becomes a living space that flexibly molds to the needs of its occupant, embodying the principles of minimalism without sacrificing comfort or style.

As morning light filters through strategically placed windows, it dances across an interior defined by practical elegance. In the kitchen, the clink of coffee mugs meets the smooth surfaces of integrated appliances and modular storage, all within arm's reach. Spatial economy is vital; everything has its place, ensuring that the limited square footage nourishes rather than constricts.

Transitioning to work, the home office, a compact nook, or a fold-down desk becomes the nexus of productivity. Here, connectivity to the digital realm is seamless, and the presence of technology is hidden. The acoustic considerations of the container's build mean that conference calls are insulated from the outside world's hum, creating an oasis of concentration.

Daylight cascades across multifunctional spaces that change with the sun's arc, transforming from home offices to yoga studios and then to gathering spots for evening entertainment. Sliding doors and convertible furniture pieces allow the inhabitant to sculpt the space to the moment's needs, crafting a dynamic environment that is ever-responsive.

The spatial constraints inherent in a container home encourage a lifestyle unburdened by excess. Here, possessions are curated, each item intentionally selected for its utility or emotional value. The home becomes a gallery, not of opulence, but of essentialism, where each element serves a purpose, contributing to the home's collective character.

In this life, the interplay with the outdoors is fundamental. Decks and patio areas extend the living space, blurring the lines between inside and outside. Container homes, often fitted with large glass doors, invite the outdoors in, promoting a lifestyle that acknowledges the importance of nature's therapeutic effects. Urban container homes make a virtue of their setting, with rooftop gardens and balcony planters contributing to an eco-friendly footprint and providing a personal retreat.

Evenings in a container home are a time of serenity. Energy-efficient LED lighting softens the industrial edges, and well-insulated walls keep the bustle of the city at bay. The compact dimensions promote intimacy, turning what could be a limitation into an opportunity for closeness and conversation.

Energy conservation is not an abstract concept but a tangible feature of daily life. From solar panels that power the home to water-saving fixtures that speak to environmental stewardship, the functionality of the container home is intrinsically linked to a sustainable lifestyle. The architect, as an inhabitant, understands that these features are not just conveniences but commitments to a philosophy that values resourcefulness and respect for the planet.

Maintenance, often a laborious aspect of homeownership, is streamlined in a container home. Durable materials and innovative design mean that upkeeping the home is not a chore but a pleasure, a matter of pride in the stewardship of a space that stands as a testament to ingenuity and foresight.

In a container home, daily life is not a series of tasks but a seamless experience of living in sync with one's values. It's a life of engagement with the present and a conscious step towards a sustainable future. For the urban architect, a container home is both a personal sanctuary and a professional beacon, a demonstration of what is possible when innovation is applied with intent and an eye toward functionality.

In closing, life in a container home is a rhythm paced by the efficiency of design and the cadence of sustainable habits. It's a reflection of a mindset that sees beyond the conventional, embracing a lifestyle that is both a statement and a solution, resonating with the forward-thinking individual who finds beauty in simplicity and sophistication in functionality.

Community and Neighbours

Embracing a container home is much like composing a piece of music where each note contributes to a grander melody. This melody harmonizes the life of an architect with their community, each shipping container home adding a distinct resonance to the urban symphony.

For the architect, the container home isn't merely a personal stronghold; it's the nexus of their professional and personal ethos. This form of living doesn't isolate, but rather, it integrates, weaving into the social and cultural fabric of the neighborhood. In the eclectic urban sprawl where every inch of space is at a premium, container homes stand out with their unconventional charm, becoming landmarks of innovation and practical aesthetics.

The inhabitants of these homes, including the architects themselves, are often seen as mavericks. Yet, their very presence invites a broader discussion about space utilization, sustainability, and the future of urban housing. They are not outliers but connectors, bridging diverse groups with their shared interest in responsible living. Here, an architect's home may serve as a community classroom, an informal gathering place where the conversation turns naturally towards responsible urban development and the potential of minimalistic lifestyles.

Moreover, container homes often attract those who espouse a minimalist and sustainable lifestyle, setting the stage for a neighborhood characterized by shared values. The communal spirit in such areas is palpable, with neighbors uniting over urban gardening projects, energy co-operatives, and local sustainability workshops. This is not just about neighborliness; it's about constructing a collective vision for a loveable future.

The integration of these homes into existing neighborhoods serves as a catalyst for engagement. Architects are uniquely positioned to spearhead initiatives that mesh their innovative homes into the fabric of the city. Such efforts can elevate the profile of the community, drawing in investment and interest, which can spark revitalization efforts. This symbiosis between the home and the neighborhood is a testament to the architect's role, not just as a builder of structures but as a weaver of communities.

Container homes, with their modularity and adaptability, can be arranged to foster interaction and camaraderie among neighbors. Shared spaces become hubs of activity, promoting a sense of belonging and mutual support that might be absent in traditional urban living scenarios. For the resident architect, such an environment is both a living lab and a showcase, offering daily insights into the interplay between design, functionality, and social dynamics.

Living in a container home can transform the architect into a community figure, someone who represents the forward-thinking, environmentally conscious spirit of the neighborhood. The professional and the private meld, as the home becomes both a personal sanctuary and a public statement. It's not uncommon for architects to invite the community into their homes, using them as galleries of possibility, promoting dialogue on sustainable living and innovative architectural practices.

The neighborhood itself, dotted with container homes, morphs into a microcosm of what the future urban landscape could become. It's a place where innovation isn't just tolerated; it's the norm. Such spaces challenge the status quo and offer a template for living that others in the city may wish to emulate.

For those within the community, the presence of container homes and their inhabitants serves as a daily reminder of the potential that lies in thinking differently about our spaces. They foster an environment where the values of sustainability and minimalism are not just idle talk but are lived experiences. They create an ambiance where the architect's role transcends the conventional, where their work and life become interconnected pieces of the community puzzle.

In conclusion, the life of an architect in a container home is a statement of both personal belief and professional ambition. It's a tangible expression of a commitment to a lifestyle that values sustainability, innovation, and community. This commitment is not made in isolation but is instead a chord struck in harmony with the surrounding urban fabric, resonating with the collective rhythm of the community. Through living in such homes, architects can connect with like-minded individuals, inspire change, and take an active role in shaping the society they inhabit. The container home becomes more than a residence—it becomes a vessel for community building, a cornerstone for neighborhood cohesion, and a beacon for the architectural future.

Chapter 16

Maintenance and Upkeep

Routine Maintenance Checklist

In the realm of shipping container homes, the allure of sustainability and innovation is met with the pragmatism of maintenance. Maintenance is the rhythmical heartbeat of a container home's longevity, a practice not unlike the care a musician bestows upon their cherished instrument, ensuring that its music remains timeless.

As architects, our relationship with our creations doesn't end upon their inception. We inhabit them, and thus, the need to keep them vibrant and robust is both a professional necessity and a personal endeavor. In the ensuing lines, we will unfold the tapestry of routine maintenance for a container home. This dwelling, by its nature, defies convention yet subscribes to the universal creed of care.

Firstly, the shell, that corrugated expanse of steel that both defines and shelters, demands vigilance against corrosion. This nemesis of metal is combated not through sporadic attention but through a ritualistic calendar of inspection and touch-up painting. Bi-annual examinations of the exterior, mainly after the harsher climes of winter and the searing tests of summer, will disclose any rust spots or paint failures that necessitate swift action. The choice of high-quality, rust-inhibitive paint is more than an aesthetic preference; it's a barrier against the relentless elements.

Moving to the joints and seams, those critical points where materials meet and where vulnerabilities might lie, a discerning eye must assess the caulking. The integrity of these seals ensures the home remains impervious to moisture – the silent invader that can warp, rot, and undermine. The caulking should be reviewed with the change of seasons, making repairs as needed to sustain the home's hermetic peace.

Within, the internal checks are no less vital. The dynamic interplay of indoor air quality and ventilation forms a crucial chapter in maintenance. Regularly replacing filters in your HVAC system and ensuring vents remain unblocked and functional curtails the accumulation of dampness and mold, those insidious foes of a healthful living environment.

Electrical systems, the veined network that empowers the home, require an annual review by a qualified electrician. This check will ensure that all components are functioning correctly and are up to code, forestalling any potential hazards that lie in neglect.

Plumbing, that vital circulatory system, must flow unimpeded. Regularly scheduled descaling, mainly if your home is in a region with hard water, extends the lifespan of your pipes and fixtures. Inspection for leaks under sinks and around toilets should become a monthly ritual, for water's destructive power belies its life-giving nature.

The undercarriage, often an overlooked aspect of a container home, should be scrutinized semi-annually. This inspection is to ensure the integrity of the insulation and the absence of pest infestations or water damage, which can go unnoticed until they burgeon into critical issues.

A container home's roof, the unsung hero bearing the brunt of sun, rain, and debris, requires a bi-annual audit. The removal of debris and the assessment of any pooling water will forestall the degradation of its surface.

And let us not neglect the operational elements – doors and windows. Their regular use begets wear, and thus, hinges and seals should be checked and maintained to ensure they function with ease and efficiency.

Lastly, as seasons turn, the land upon which the home sits must be considered. Drainage is paramount; water must be guided away from the dwelling to defend against the undermining of foundations and the insidious seepage into the structure. Landscaping, therefore, is not merely an aesthetic endeavor but a sentinel against the elements, requiring seasonal adjustment and maintenance.

In conclusion, the routine maintenance of a container home is a tapestry of tasks, a symphony of care that ensures the health and longevity of the dwelling. For the architect, these acts of upkeep are not mundane chores but a manifestation of respect for the design and a commitment to sustainability. Inhabiting such a space compels us to become custodians of a future vision, living out the promise of innovation with every attentive act of maintenance. Through diligence and care, the container home transcends its materials to become a lasting, living testament to the principles of minimalism and sustainable living that we hold dear.

Longevity of Container Homes

The interplay between form and time has always fascinated those who create. For architects, the aspiration isn't merely to design structures that inspire but to erect beacons of durability capable of transcending the ephemeral. When the subject of conversation turns to the longevity of container homes, we enter a realm where ingenuity collides with the relentless tide of time.

Container homes, robust in their infancy as vessels of global trade, possess an intrinsic durability. Their second incarnation as homes is both a testament to human resourcefulness and a challenge to their lifespan. How long can these steel sanctuaries withstand the relentless march of the years? The answer lies not in a simple figure but in a narrative of care, adaptation, and perpetual vigilance.

At the heart of a container home's longevity is its resistance to the elements. When shielded with appropriate insulation and protective coatings, the container laughs in the face of both sweltering heat and biting cold. These are not temporary shelters but potentially lifelong homes, with some estimates placing their lifespan at a formidable 50 years or more, assuming they're maintained with the respect they deserve.

The skeletal strength of a container home is unquestionable. Corten steel, the material of choice for these containers, is a wonder in itself, designed to weather the storm and emerge with a patina that speaks of resilience rather than decay. When architects and homeowners approach these structures with reverence for their innate strength, container homes become less about transient dwellings and more about enduring habitation.

Yet, no material, no matter how formidable, is unbeatable. The marine-grade paint that initially coats the containers is just the starting point. Homeowners must engage in a symphony of upkeep, where the repainting of exterior surfaces is as much a rite as it is a requirement. The selection of paint, always with an eye towards environmental compatibility and longevity, becomes an essential chapter in the life story of the container home.

What of the welds and joins, the stitches that hold the steel fabric together? Here, vigilant inspection and prompt action can prevent the minutest breach from becoming a gaping wound. The joining of separate containers, a dance of precision and expertise, sets the stage for a structure that can proudly endure the test of time.

The environmental credentials of container homes are more than a selling point; they're a pledge toward sustainability. The insulation choices, critical to energy efficiency, also play a pivotal role in preserving the integrity of the container against internal condensation – the silent adversary of longevity. A well-insulated container home remains temperate and dry, its internal climate controlled, and its fabric unspoiled.

While the steel structure may be the bones of the home, the systems within are its lifeblood. Plumbing, electrical, and HVAC systems need the same foresight applied to the exterior. High-quality fixtures and regular maintenance aren't mere additions; they're integral to the home's enduring function.

Even as the steel resists, the foundation must hold. The strategic engineering of the foundation, designed to buffer against shifting soils and creeping moisture, ensures the home remains steadfast. Here, the connection between the container and the earth is more than structural; it's foundational to the longevity of the home.

As with all things, adaptation is crucial to survival. A container home is not static; it evolves with the needs and technologies of the time. Upgrades to fixtures, fittings, and energy systems are not just improvements but lifelines, extending the home's relevance and durability.

Beyond the tangible, the spirit of the home contributes to its longevity. A container home that is loved and resonates with the lives within is maintained not out of duty but devotion. These homes, born from a desire for sustainability and simplicity, find their place in the narratives of their inhabitants, and in those stories, they find their immortality.

In summation, the longevity of a container home is a chronicle of care, adaptation, and respect for the materials from which it is crafted. With mindful maintenance and an embrace of sustainable living, these homes stand not as temporary abodes but as legacies of architectural foresight. They become less about the novelty of their form and more about their role as enduring sanctuaries, standing resolute against the passage of time, embodying the principles of an architectural practice that is as timeless as the structures it seeks to create.

Chapter 17

Expanding Your Container Home

Planning Additions

In the vibrant symphony of building, the act of expanding a home is a movement that demands both the foresight of a conductor and the precision of a virtuoso. The canvas of container homes, with their modular majesty, invites a unique opportunity for architects: the ability to expand living space in ways traditional structures may not permit. It is a narrative not just of adding space but of augmenting a story, of composing new chapters in the lives that unfold within its metallic embrace.

When planning additions to a container home, the architect becomes both the weaver of dreams and the steward of practicality. The vision begins with an understanding that these steel modules, once purposed for the high seas, now serve a new quest for space, sustainability, and sophistication. The process is a delicate balance between the dreams of expansion and the physics of reality, between the desires of the heart and the demands of the land.

The initial sketches that dance across the drawing board are not mere lines and angles; they are the silent language of potential. An addition must do more than provide more area—it must integrate seamlessly with the existing structure, maintaining the integrity of design and the spirit of innovation that is the hallmark of container living. As the architect, your every stroke is a dialogue between your vision and the rigid yet remarkably adaptable nature of container construction.

Understanding the symbiotic relationship between the new and the old is paramount. Additions are not just bolted-on appendages; they must be a natural progression, a harmonious blending of spaces that respects the original aesthetic while amplifying its function. The choice of where to join a new container, how to create flow between old and new spaces, and the way light and air will traverse the expanded environment are considerations that echo the soul of architectural artistry.

In expanding a container home, one must also consult the silent partner in every construction: the land itself. Your extension's foundation does not simply support weight; it anchors dreams to the earth, demanding the same attention to detail as the original construction. The soil must be understood, respected, and prepared to bear the weight of new aspirations.

With a foundation of understanding, the walls can rise. Here, the architect's skill is measured in the ability to foresee the dance between existing and new materials. The addition must be woven into the fabric of the home with the precision of a master tailor. It involves not just technical prowess in joining and insulating containers but an innate sense of aesthetics. The material continuity, the flow of interior and exterior design, must be seamless, creating an expansion that feels as though it was always meant to be.

The interior of the new space is where the architect's touch turns from the structural to the sublime. How will the space be used? What stories will unfold within its confines? The design must cater not just to the practicalities of living but to the nuances of life's ever-changing rhythm. It is here, in the planning of living areas, workspaces, or creative studios, that the addition truly becomes a home.

Finally, in the symphony of expansion, the crescendo is reached with the orchestration of systems. Plumbing, electrical, and HVAC must be integrated into the new addition with both technical skill and an eye toward future advancements. These veins and arteries of the home must be laid with the understanding that they are the lifelines of comfort and functionality.

In the quiet aftermath, as the dust settles and the sound of construction fades, the addition stands not just as a testament to the home's physical growth but to the evolution of the architect's journey. It is a hallmark of your ability to blend the robust, industrial heritage of shipping containers with the finesse of modern design.

The expansion of a container home is a challenge, a joy, and a responsibility—an opportunity to redefine the boundaries of modular living while paying homage to the pioneering spirit that is at the core of the container home movement. Each addition is a legacy, a physical embodiment of the principle that life, like architecture, is an ever-evolving art.

Connecting Multiple Containers

When we talk about the expansion of a container home, specifically the art of connecting multiple containers, we delve into a topic that is as much about engineering as it is about creativity. The process is an intricate dance of form and function, a harmonious blend of aesthetics and pragmatism. The vision for connecting these steel modules transcends their utilitarian origins, transforming them into fluid and interconnected living spaces that captivate the imagination and serve the practical needs of their inhabitants.

The narrative begins with a single container, standing solitary, and its stories etched into corrugated walls that once cut through stormy seas. The expansion process introduces companions to this narrative—additional containers that will bond with the original, not just by the might of welds and fastenings, but through the cohesive vision of an architect who understands the depth of potential that lies within.

In this endeavor, the connection points are pivotal. They're the physical embodiment of design decisions, serving as the conduits through which the home's lifeblood—its people—will flow. These junctions of steel are crafted with precision, allowing for the movement and interaction that transforms a structure into a home. The connections determine the rhythm of daily life, guiding residents from one room to the next, from solitude to gathering, from rest to activity.

Yet, as these containers join, the architect faces the challenge of blending the individual characteristics of each unit into a seamless whole. This is where the understanding of space and flow comes into play, arranging the containers not just for maximum utility but also for the aesthetic dialogue they foster with their occupants and the environment. The challenge is to celebrate the individuality of each container while achieving a unified structure that feels preordained and intentional.

The exterior of this composite structure must be addressed with an artistic eye and practical hand. Each container's journey and narrative are honored while being brought into a cohesive architectural language that speaks to the structure's new purpose. This includes the choice of cladding materials, the interplay of light and shadow, and the incorporation of environmental features like green roofs or solar panels—all elements that must be harmonized to present an inviting and sustainable abode.

Internally, as the walls of these robust containers merge, the internal space becomes a canvas for the architect's design ethos. The interior must not only be visually pleasing but must also function seamlessly. The placement of openings, the flow of light, the choice of finishes—all these elements require meticulous planning to ensure the space is practical, durable and imbued with a sense of peace and comfort.

Beneath the visual aesthetic lies the symphony of systems—electrical, plumbing, and HVAC—that must be masterfully orchestrated to function without intrusion. These systems are integrated within the structure with an eye for efficiency and accessibility, ensuring the home operates as a single, cohesive unit. The challenge lies in threading these vital systems through the containers without compromising on the integrity and form of the design.

In the grand composition of connecting multiple containers, the facade presents a critical final touch. The exterior must resonate with the innovative spirit of container architecture yet stand as a unified front, a declaration of a home that is as unique as its inhabitants. This is where the materials, textures, and colors come into their own, as the architect dresses the structure to reflect the values and stories of those who will dwell within.

Upon completion, the structure stands as more than a mere collection of containers. It is a home, an architectural achievement that represents the zenith of modern, sustainable living. It is a testament to the possibilities that emerge when imagination is applied to modular elements, a showcase of the beauty that arises from the union of individual components into a symphony of residential design.

For the architect, this endeavor is not just a matter of connecting disparate pieces; it is about creating a living, breathing space that embodies the principles of modernity, sustainability, and minimalism. It is a reflection of a career devoted to innovation, a tangible expression of a life's work in creating homes that are not only structures of refuge but are emblematic of a commitment to a future where design thinks beyond the confines of tradition. This is the journey of connecting multiple containers: a story of creation, innovation, and the indefatigable human spirit that finds a home within the steel.

Chapter 18

Case Studies

Inspirational Examples

Amidst the steel canvas of urban sprawl, architects like you, driven by a passion for sustainability and innovation, have long sought the balance between practical need and artistic expression. You stand on the precipice of a decision to integrate shipping container homes into your practice. In this chapter, we explore inspirational examples that have transcended the typical bounds of architecture and have, in their way, redefined the concept of home.

The Eclectic Marvel: The New Orleans Gem

Consider the story of a home in New Orleans, where vibrant culture and the necessity of resilience post-Katrina merged to create an eclectic marvel. Here, a container home rose not just as a solution to housing but as a beacon of ingenuity and adaptability. Multiple containers were tessellated to form a two-story structure that challenges the very notion of post-disaster rebuilding. The exterior, painted with murals reflective of the city's rich artistic heritage, stands as a testament to the community's indomitable spirit. At the same time, its solar-paneled roof speaks to a commitment to sustainable living.

The Modular Retreat: California's Haven

Move then to the rolling hills of California, where a tech entrepreneur sought solace away from the silicon buzz. In this sanctuary, shipping containers become luxurious retreats, each positioned to capitalize on the stunning vistas and natural light. The interior showcases a minimalist approach, where less becomes more, and simplicity reigns. Here, the containers are a retreat, proving that luxury need not be expansive but can be contained within the bounds of reasonable space usage and intentional design.

The Urban Tapestry: A Brooklyn Brownstone

In Brooklyn, where historical brownstones line the streets, a container home has been woven into the urban fabric. A young architectural collective reimagined what a Brooklyn home could be, using containers to add a modern touch to the traditional aesthetic. The result is a home that respects its historical context while boldly asserting its place in the architectural landscape of tomorrow. Its rooftop garden offers a green respite in the concrete jungle, reminding us that even in the densest of habitats, nature can be nurtured.

The Community Mosaic: Amsterdam's Social Experiment

Across the ocean, in Amsterdam, a social experiment took shape in the form of a container housing project. This venture was more than a housing solution; it was a deliberate act of community building. Each unit, although identical in structure, became unique through the personalization of its residents. This development was not just about creating affordable housing; it was about crafting a mosaic of individual spaces that come together to form a vibrant and supportive community.

The Remote Homestead: The Patagonian Escape

Venture further to the rugged landscapes of Patagonia, where a remote container home stands against the backdrop of towering mountains. Here, the challenge was not just aesthetic but environmental. The containers were retrofitted to withstand the harsh climate, their exteriors fortified, and their interiors transformed into warm, wood-lined sanctuaries. This home is not just a place of dwelling but a fortress of solitude, proving that container homes can thrive even in the most unforgiving environments.

The Suburban Prototype: An Australian Experiment

In the suburbs of Melbourne, Australia, an architect saw potential in the unassuming container to shake up suburban monotony. The resulting home breaks the mold of the typical suburban home with its bold geometry and sustainable features, becoming a prototype for future developments. This home challenges the status quo, demonstrating that innovation can find its place in even the most established of settings.

Each of these examples serves as a beacon, guiding you through the myriad possibilities that container homes present. They are proof of concept that within the confines of corrugated steel walls lies the potential for unbounded creativity. These homes are not just structures; they are living, breathing entities that have captured the essence of their inhabitants' values and ethos.

As you embark on incorporating shipping container homes into your architectural practice, let these case studies remind you that you are part of a grand tradition of innovation. You are not just building homes; you are crafting legacies. These inspirational examples are your kin, your community of forward-thinkers who see the potential for a shipping container to be much more than a vessel for cargo— it can be a vessel for life.

Lessons Learned from Experienced Owners

In the realm of shipping container home construction and habitation, the collected wisdom of those who have undertaken this unique approach to living is a tapestry of stories, advice, and cautionary tales. This section delves deep into the hearts and minds of experienced container homeowners, weaving their singular threads of experience into a rich, instructive narrative for the modern architect who dares to dream differently.

At its core, the philosophy of the container home enthusiast is predicated on a marriage between functionality and aesthetics. These steel structures, once the vessels of international trade, have been lovingly, though pragmatically, transformed into living spaces that challenge the conventions of traditional architecture. The container home is not merely a residence; it's a living sculpture that is inhabited by a daily encounter between human aspiration and industrial minimalism. The seasoned advice of owners whispers a truth about these homes: they demand an aesthetic that honors the robustness of their material yet invites the softness of human touch, a mingling of the organic with the manufactured.

Owners reflect on the container's essence, an intangible quality that transcends its physical boundaries. There's a reverence for the container's original form, and successful transformations are those that tread lightly, maintaining the integrity of the container while also allowing for the expression of personal style and needs. Modifying these metal boxes is seen not as a conquest but as a collaboration between their industrial heritage and their new lease on life as comfortable, eco-conscious homes.

Climatic adaptability is another chapter in the container home story. These structures, when left unmodified, are mere conductors to the whims of the weather. Thus, the integration of climate control measures is a significant focus for those who inhabit them. Lessons from the field speak of insulation—not just the type that fills the gaps but also the kind that reflects the sun's harshness or invites a breeze to meander through open spaces. The interplay of container home design with its environment is a dance that requires both foresight and creativity.

The maximization of space is a recurring theme. These homes teach us the value of innovative thought—every square inch serves a purpose, and flexibility is king. Inhabitants speak of furniture that folds away, storage that doubles as art, and rooms that can change function with the slide of a door or the fold of a wall. It's a renaissance of space utilization, one that challenges the architect to think beyond traditional confines and imagine a home that adapts to the moment's needs.

Foundation, both literal and metaphorical, is pivotal. Owners talk about the foundational phase of building with a reverence typically reserved for sacred rituals. It's here that due diligence in planning, compliance, and research pays off, preventing the ground from shifting underfoot, both in terms of building stability and regulatory compliance. A container home's success is as much a result of its physical base as the strength of its conception and the thoroughness of its planning.

Engaging with the community emerges as a theme akin to an educational mission. Container homes, often the outliers in residential neighborhoods, serve as beacons of innovation and sustainability. Owners become de facto diplomats, bridging the gap between conventional housing and this avant-garde approach. Through transparency, dialogue, and education, they transform initial skepticism into a shared vision of a sustainable architectural future.

Sustainability is a term that has rippled through the narratives of container homeowners. They extend their meaning beyond the repurposing of materials to embody a philosophy that encompasses the lifecycle of the home and the daily practices of its inhabitants. It's about creating a living ecosystem that thrives on renewable energy, sustainable practices, and a profound connection with its environment.

Lastly, flexibility for the future is woven through every tale of container living. Owners speak to the adaptability of these structures and how their homes have grown and shifted with life's ebbs and flows. They advocate for a design philosophy that anticipates change that allows for expansion, retraction, and evolution, mirroring the dynamic nature of life itself.

These lessons, distilled from the lived experiences of container home pioneers, form a guidebook for architects and dreamers alike. They tell us that building a container home is more than a construction project; it's an exercise in imagination, a redefinition of space, and a commitment to sustainable living. With these insights, you are armed not just with knowledge but with the foresight and empathy necessary to create spaces that are not just built but are genuinely lived in.

Chapter 19

Costs and Budgeting

Estimating Your Costs

In the sprawling tapestry of urban architecture, the integration of shipping container homes is a bold stroke of ingenuity, a testament to an architect's commitment to sustainability and innovation. The journey from concept to completion is a delicate interplay between visionary design and economic pragmatism. Estimating costs for such a pioneering endeavor is as much about understanding the nuances of the market as it is about grasping the physical materials that will embody your architectural aspirations.

Begin with the containers themselves, the bedrock of your project. Their acquisition is not a simple transaction but a strategic engagement with the fluctuating market. Prices are as diverse as the containers' past voyages, influenced by their condition, size, and proximity to your site. The astute architect navigates these waters with a keen eye, knowing that suitable containers at the right price can set the stage for the entire project's financial framework.

From this foundation, you must chart the course of design and planning. This stage is more alchemy than science, where every line drawn in the blueprint has cost implications. Your design expertise is the key here, transforming steel boxes into a harmonious living space. It is where aesthetic appeal and functionality merge, and while this phase demands a considerable time investment, it pays dividends by preempting construction complexities that can inflate budgets unexpectedly.

As you prepare your urban canvas, the site itself demands attention. Every city lot comes with its personality, a set of challenges and opportunities that will influence your project's bottom line. It would be best if you considered the costs of excavation, grading, and laying foundations—all under the watchful eye of urban regulations that govern land use and impact the financial outlay.

The assembly of your container home is the crescendo, where the physical transformation occurs. Here, labor costs converge with material expenses. The complexity of your design will be echoed in the labor hours required, and every modification—from cutting windows to reinforcing walls—adds to the financial narrative. The choice of sustainable options, while potentially higher in immediate costs, can lead to long-term savings, underscoring the importance of an architect's foresight in planning.

Interior and exterior finishes articulate the final character of your creation. They are the visible expressions of your architectural intent and the homeowner's personality. This stage is a complex variable in your cost estimation, impacted by the choice of materials, fixtures, and fittings that range from the economical to the extravagant. Your design must mediate between durability, aesthetic value, and the ever-present budget constraints.

Less tangible but equally critical are the permits and legalities, the silent partners in your construction concerto. The expense of navigating this labyrinth of regulations is an unavoidable chapter in your cost estimation narrative. Building codes, zoning laws, and the necessary permits shape the project, ensuring that your structure is not only innovative but compliant.

In conclusion, estimating the costs of a shipping container home in an urban setting is to embark on a narrative that is complex and multifaceted. It's about making informed predictions, taking educated risks, and being ready to adapt. Each container home tells a story of its own, with a budget that reflects its unique plotline, shaped by the market's moods, the site's characteristics, and the creative dialogue between architect and client. Your role is to be the author of this story, penning a tale not only of construction but of sustainable living and economic understanding, crafting a home that stands as a paragon of innovative urban dwelling.

Financing Your Container Home

In the ever-evolving field of architecture, particularly for those enchanted by the allure of sustainability and innovation, the concept of a container home transcends mere living space. It becomes a reflection of personal ethos and professional ambition. As an architect nestled in the prime of your career, with a penchant for minimalism and sustainable living, the journey to finance a container home is as much a testament to your creativity as your designs are. This comprehensive guide aims to navigate the unique financial pathways and strategies integral to transforming your vision of a container home into a tangible reality.

Navigating the Financial Terrain

The financial landscape for a container home project diverges significantly from traditional home financing due to its unconventional nature. Standard mortgage options might only sometimes align with the unique facets of container homes, steering you toward more innovative financing solutions. Your role as an architect, known for thinking outside the box, becomes crucial in this regard.

Exploring alternative lending sources such as personal loans, peer-to-peer lending platforms, and credit unions can open doors that traditional banks might not. These institutions are often more adaptable and willing to finance projects that break the mold, like container homes. Their flexibility can be a significant advantage in funding your unique architectural project.

Green loans and incentives should also be a focal point in your financing strategy. As an architect committed to eco-friendly practices, these loans, geared explicitly towards sustainable projects, can offer more favorable terms, including lower interest rates or rebates. Delving into local and federal incentives for sustainable building can further bolster your financial plan, providing support or tax benefits for your environmentally conscious endeavor.

Private investors and crowdfunding are avenues worth considering. The uniqueness of your project – a blend of state-of-the-art architecture and environmental stewardship – has the potential to draw the attention of investors interested in green building initiatives. Crowdfunding, on the other hand, taps into a community that values sustainability and innovative housing solutions, providing a platform to raise funds while simultaneously increasing public awareness of your project.

Detailed Budgeting: The Blueprint of Financial Success

The precision and attention to detail you apply in your architectural blueprints are equally essential in crafting your financial plan. A comprehensive assessment of all potential costs forms the foundation of this plan. This includes acquiring containers, site preparation, modifications, interior design, and a contingency fund for unexpected expenses – a common occurrence in customized projects like container homes.

Adopting a phased financing approach can make the process more manageable. By segmenting the project into distinct phases and financing each separately, you maintain financial flexibility, allowing room for adjustments and adaptations as the project unfolds.

Leveraging Your Professional Standing

Your established standing and experience in the architectural community are valuable assets in this venture. These can be leveraged to negotiate better terms with suppliers and contractors, potentially reducing overall project costs. Your professional network can also be a resource for finding cost-effective solutions and even financial support.

The Showcase Project: A Financial and Professional Lever

Constructing your container home as a showcase project provides a unique opportunity. It serves as a tangible manifestation of your skills and dedication to sustainable living, potentially attracting clients interested in similar projects. This can lead to new business opportunities and an additional revenue stream, which can be reinvested into your container home, thereby supporting it financially.

Final Thoughts: A Vision Funded with Ingenuity

The process of financing a container home requires a blend of creativity, strategic planning, and the effective use of your professional skills and network. By exploring diverse financing options, meticulously planning your budget, and leveraging your project as a showcase, you can turn your vision of a sustainable, minimalist container home into reality.

This endeavor goes beyond building a residence; it's about creating a legacy in sustainable architecture. The container home stands as a symbol of the harmonious blend of your passions, professional growth, and the pursuit of sustainable living. It demonstrates how innovative design can be both practically and financially achievable, setting a new benchmark in the architectural community and inspiring others to explore similar paths. Through this project, you're not just constructing a building; you're crafting a statement about the future of living spaces, sustainability, and architectural innovation.

Chapter 20

Moving Forward

Embracing the Container Home Community

In the dynamic landscape of modern architecture, where sustainability intersects with innovative design, the container home stands as a symbol of ingenuity and ecological responsibility. As an architect in the prime of your career, deeply embedded in the ethos of minimalism and sustainability, your journey towards embracing the container home community is not just a professional endeavor but a personal pilgrimage into a world that mirrors your values and visions.

This chapter, the culmination of a journey in sustainable architecture, delves into the essence of the container home community. It's a tapestry woven from diverse threads of ideas, experiences, and aspirations, where every member contributes to the richness of this collective. The community is not limited to fellow architects and designers but extends to environmental enthusiasts, minimalist advocates, and families who have chosen container homes as their abode. It's a melting pot of perspectives, each adding depth and color to the narrative of sustainable living.

In this vibrant community, collaboration emerges as a foundational element. It's where architects, builders, residents, and enthusiasts converge, creating a synergy that transcends the traditional architect-client relationship. This collaborative spirit is evident in workshops, forums, and social media platforms, where experiences are shared, challenges are dissected, and solutions are crafted. As an architect, your participation in this community is both as a mentor and a learner, absorbing the collective wisdom and contributing your expertise.

The stories and experiences that resonate within this community are not just tales of construction and design but chronicles of challenges, innovations, and triumphs. They are narratives that showcase the versatility of container homes, from overcoming zoning challenges to integrating cutting-edge green technologies. Each story is a learning opportunity, offering insights and inspiration for your projects. These shared experiences underscore the communal nature of the container home movement, where individual journeys interweave to form a rich tapestry of collective wisdom.

In today's digital era, the container home community transcends geographical boundaries and is connected through the web of online platforms. Social media groups, forums, and virtual webinars have become pivotal in uniting enthusiasts from different parts of the world. They serve as platforms for showcasing projects, seeking advice, and celebrating successes. For you, these digital gatherings offer a panoramic view of the global container home landscape, revealing the diverse ways these structures are being envisioned and realized.

As you step forward, embracing the container home community is about more than just adopting a new architectural style; it's about joining a movement. It's a commitment to a lifestyle that values sustainability, creativity, and collaboration. Your engagement with this community is both a professional journey and a personal evolution. It's an opportunity not just to build structures but to build relationships and be part of a narrative that is redefining the boundaries of architecture and community living.

In embracing this community, you become part of a collective vision for a sustainable future. It's a future where architecture is not just about creating buildings but about fostering a sense of community and belonging. This vision is shared and shaped by the diverse experiences and insights of its members, making the community a dynamic and evolving entity.

In conclusion, embracing the container home community marks a significant milestone in your journey as an architect. It signifies your entry into a world where your professional skills and personal beliefs align in pursuit of sustainable, innovative living solutions. This community is not just about sharing knowledge and experiences; it's about building a collective future that values sustainability, innovation, and a deep sense of community. As you integrate into this community, your role transcends that of an architect; you become a visionary, a leader, and a part of a more significant movement that is shaping the future of sustainable living. This chapter, therefore, is more than just a conclusion to a book; it's an open door to a world of possibilities, an invitation to be part of a revolution in the way we think about homes, communities, and our place in the world.

The Future of Container Home Living

As we stand at the cusp of a new era in architecture, the concept of container homes emerges as a beacon of innovation and sustainability. For you, an architect deeply ingrained in the ethos of minimalist and sustainable design, container homes represent more than just an alternative living space – they symbolize a shift towards a more conscious and responsible way of life. This chapter is dedicated to exploring the future of container home living, delving into how this burgeoning trend is set to reshape our perception of architecture, community, and environmental stewardship.

The evolution of container homes is intricately tied to the growing challenges of urban living – space constraints, rising costs, and the urgent need for sustainability. These modular structures, with their inherent flexibility, offer a solution that is not just space-efficient but also aligns with the principles of eco-friendliness and minimalism. The adaptability of containers allows for an array of creative designs, making them a fitting choice for the varied landscapes of modern cities.

In the near future, technological advancements will be pivotal in the growth of container homes. Integration of smart home technologies, efficient energy systems, and renewable resources will be central to this evolution. Imagine container homes equipped with cutting-edge insulation, solar panels, and systems for rainwater harvesting, transforming them into self-sufficient units that not only provide comfort but also drastically reduce ecological footprints. The incorporation of intelligent technologies will enhance living standards while upholding the values of sustainability.

The concept of community is set to be redefined by container home living. These homes, often part of larger communal setups, will foster a sense of interconnectedness and shared values among residents. This cooperative living model will address issues of urban isolation, creating vibrant, supportive communities centered around shared resources and spaces. The future will see these communities thriving on collective responsibility and a shared commitment to environmental conservation.

As container homes gain mainstream acceptance, their future will also be shaped by regulatory bodies and governments. The establishment of specific building codes and standards will ensure safety, sustainability, and compliance. This regulatory framework will not only safeguard residents but also encourage more architects and builders to consider container homes as a viable and appealing option, leading to their broader acceptance and implementation.

Architectural innovation will remain at the heart of container home living. The unique nature of containers will inspire architects to explore new realms of aesthetic and functional design, pushing the boundaries of traditional architecture. The future will see container homes evolving into architectural statements, showcasing the creativity and vision of their designers.

Sustainability will continue to be a central theme in the narrative of container homes. Their ability to repurpose materials, combined with eco-friendly practices, positions them as a model for green living. As global awareness of environmental issues intensifies, the demand for sustainable housing solutions like container homes is expected to surge, further solidifying their role in the future of urban living.

Container home living is more than a housing trend – it's a global movement towards more conscious living. This movement transcends borders, uniting people across different cultures and backgrounds in a shared vision for a sustainable future. The future of container home living is about creating a global community that values minimalism, environmental stewardship, and innovative design.

In summary, the future of container home living is a vibrant tapestry of technological innovation, community building, regulatory evolution, architectural creativity, and unwavering commitment to sustainability. As an architect at the forefront of this movement, your role extends beyond designing structures to being an advocate for a way of life that champions sustainability and community cohesion. Container homes are set to become more than just alternative living spaces; they are poised to be symbolic of a world that values thoughtful, responsible, and innovative approaches to living. This chapter is not just a look into what lies ahead for container homes; it's an invitation to participate in a transformative journey that reimagines the essence of home, community, and our collective future.

Appendices

Resources for Further Learning

In the dynamic and ever-evolving field of container home architecture, the journey of learning and development is continuous. As an architect who embodies a passion for sustainable and innovative building practices, your quest for knowledge extends beyond the completion of a single project. This comprehensive guide is crafted to provide you with an array of resources designed to deepen your expertise, inspire creativity, and keep you abreast of the latest trends and technologies in the realm of container home living.

A Fusion of Literature, Digital Exploration, and Interactive Learning

Delving into the world of architecture literature is a fundamental step. Seek books and publications that not only discuss sustainable architecture but also dive into the specifics of container home design and construction. These texts are often a blend of theoretical knowledge and practical case studies, providing a rich understanding of the field. Simultaneously, the digital landscape offers a plethora of online platforms, such as architectural blogs, forums, and websites dedicated to container homes. These digital resources are constantly updated with the latest news, trends, and innovative ideas, making them invaluable for staying current in the field.

Interactive learning through workshops, seminars, and conferences is equally vital. These events offer direct insights from leading experts and provide a platform for networking with other professionals. They serve as a nexus for knowledge exchange, where real-world challenges and innovative solutions are shared. Engaging in these interactive experiences not only enhances your professional knowledge but also fosters connections that could lead to future collaborations and projects.

Embracing Technology and Community Engagement

In today's world, mastering architectural software and tools is crucial for translating creative visions into tangible designs. Familiarizing yourself with the latest 3D modeling, energy efficiency simulation, and structural analysis software can significantly enhance the design and execution of your container home projects. These tools not only aid in creating efficient and sustainable designs but also ensure that your creations are aesthetically compelling and practical.

Furthermore, immersing yourself in communities and groups focused on container home living and sustainable architecture can be profoundly enriching. These platforms offer a space for sharing experiences, engaging in discussions, and collaborating on projects. The collective wisdom and diverse perspectives found in these communities can inspire new ideas and provide practical solutions to common challenges.

Sustainable Materials Research and Reflective Practice

Staying informed about sustainable materials and emerging technologies is essential for an architect focusing on eco-friendly practices. Researching sustainable insulation options, renewable energy sources, and environmentally friendly interior materials can significantly enhance the sustainability quotient of your projects. Keeping abreast of these developments allows you to integrate advanced, eco-conscious solutions into your designs, aligning with your commitment to sustainability.

In addition to external resources, reflective practice is a powerful tool for personal and professional growth. Documenting your own projects, reflecting on the challenges encountered, and analyzing the solutions and outcomes provide invaluable insights. This personal record not only serves as a testament to your professional journey but also becomes a practical guide for future endeavors, capturing the unique experiences and learnings that each project brings.

Conclusion: A Journey of Continuous Growth and Inspiration

The resources available for further learning in container home architecture are diverse and comprehensive, encompassing literature, digital media, interactive events, technology, community involvement, sustainable materials research, and personal reflection. Each of these resources offers unique insights and contributes to your growth as an architect committed to innovative and sustainable practices. This journey of continuous learning is not just about acquiring knowledge; it's about shaping a future where architecture resonates with your values of sustainability, innovation, and community impact. As you delve into these resources, remember that each step taken is a stride towards redefining the possibilities in the world of container home living and sustainable architecture.

Glossary

Architectural and Construction Terms.

Container Modification: Refers to the alterations made to shipping containers to make them suitable for habitation. This includes structural changes, cutting for windows and doors, and interior modifications.

Off-grid Systems: Systems that allow the container home to operate independently of the traditional utility grid. This includes solar power systems, rainwater harvesting setups, and composting toilets.

Passive Solar Design: A design principle that harnesses the sun's energy for heating and cooling, reducing reliance on artificial systems. Involves strategic placement of windows and use of materials to absorb and distribute solar heat.

R-value: A measure of insulation's ability to resist heat flow. Higher R-values indicate more effective insulation, a critical aspect in container homes for energy efficiency and comfort.

Structural Integrity: Refers to the strength and durability of the container structure, especially after modifications. It's vital to maintain the container's structural integrity for safety and longevity.

Design and Aesthetics.

Cladding Options: Materials used to cover the exterior of a container home for aesthetic appeal and additional insulation. Common choices include wood, metal, and composite materials.

Multifunctional Furniture: Furniture designed to serve multiple purposes, maximizing space usage within the compact interior of a container home. Examples include beds with built-in storage or foldable dining tables.

Open-plan Layout: An interior design approach where walls are minimized to create open, interconnected living spaces. Popular in container homes for a more spacious feel.

Environmental and Sustainability Terms.

Eco-friendly Materials: Building materials that have a low impact on the environment, either through sustainable sourcing, low emissions, or recyclability. Essential in container homes for minimizing ecological footprints.

HVAC Options: Heating, Ventilation, and Air Conditioning systems suited for container homes, often focusing on energy efficiency and compactness.

Sustainable Landscape Design: The practice of designing environmentally sustainable outdoor spaces, often incorporating native plants, water-efficient gardens, and permaculture principles.

Legal and Regulatory Terms.

Building Codes and Compliance: Regulations set by local governments regarding the construction and modification of buildings, including container homes. Compliance is crucial for legal and safety reasons.

Zoning Laws: Legal regulations determine how land can be used in different areas, which can affect the placement and design of container homes.

Personal and Community Aspects.

Community Engagement: Involvement in local or online communities related to container homes, where experiences, advice, and support are shared.

Maintenance Checklist: A comprehensive list of routine tasks and inspections to ensure the long-term upkeep and safety of a container home.

This glossary, while not exhaustive, covers a broad spectrum of terms that are fundamental to the field of container home architecture. It serves as a foundational tool to deepen your understanding and enhance your proficiency in this specialized area. As you continue to explore and innovate within the realm of container homes, this glossary will be a valuable reference, aiding in the articulation and realization of your sustainable architectural visions.

About the Author

The author of this work for three decades has worked as Marketing Director in a variety of companies operating in the BTB Distribution of products and services in the vast IT landscape, helping to bring one of these companies to life by taking on the role of CEO.

However, his story goes far beyond the mere confines of the professional sphere.

In fact, in parallel with his tireless efforts in business, he has ardently embraced an esoteric path, becoming a Sannyasin, a devoted follower of the visionary spiritual philosopher Osho. This path of soul-searching sharpened his understanding of life, love and awareness, opening the door to deeper dimensions of human existence.

Many years of his life were devoted to meditative practice in many forms, with a particular affection for shamanism, an ancient way of connecting with nature and the spiritual world. As a "pipe bearer," he was the keeper of a sacred pipe, sharing it in the various rituals celebrated around the fire, thus symbolizing his deep connection with tradition and spirituality.

The author also officiated at numerous ceremonies inside sweat lodges, sharing with others his deep reverence for the wisdom enshrined in these ancient rituals, and his deep connection with nature.

With extraordinary skill, the author blends the richness of experience in the business world with a deep understanding of spirituality and mindfulness, offering readers a unique and enriching perspective within this work.

SW Prem Jaganu

Made in the USA
Las Vegas, NV
10 January 2024

84169878R00083